The D Project

Accelerating progress towards an inclusive culture in the investment and savings industry

Steve Butler

In early 2016, a group of leaders in the investment and savings profession met and concluded that future success for their clients, members, employers and shareholders requires a diverse and inclusive culture, and that the sector was lagging behind others in reflecting our society.

That led to the creation of The Diversity Project: a cross-company initiative whose purpose is to champion and accelerate progress towards a more inclusive culture. This book recounts the progress made to date, discusses the progress that still needs to be made and sets out practical ways to achieve it.

The Diversity Project Manifesto

We believe that we have an extraordinary opportunity to press the reset button in our industry: to recruit, nurture and retain the first truly diverse generation of investment and savings professionals.

That generation will themselves perpetuate diversity in our industry; we are looking to break one cycle and create another. If we are successful:

1. Our businesses will better reflect both society at large, and the individuals who trust us with their money.

2. Our people will create better financial outcomes to benefit our diverse savers and investors.

3. We will attract more interest in the industry, with a pipeline of diverse talent.

Diversity is not only our social obligation. It is a business imperative.

All the interviews for this book were conducted in the spring and early summer of 2020. For the most recent developments by the Diversity Project please visit:

www.diversityproject.com

Foreword
by Baroness Helena Morrissey DBE

Five years ago, the Diversity Project set out to achieve what seemed quite a simple ambition: to accelerate progress towards a more inclusive culture and greater diversity of talent in the rather traditional asset management industry. It's been quite a journey already! And it's now abundantly clear that the mission is not so simple after all. Culture is hard to change and diverse talent is hard to recruit and retain.

At the same time the case for a more modern, more diverse investment industry has never been stronger or more accepted. It's now widely acknowledged that we need diversity of thought to reach the right answers to complex problems and diversity of talent to connect better with clients and future proof the industry. Over 70 firms, 40 partner organisations and 400 people are committed to the Project, including thirty CEOs who form the Diversity Project's Advisory Council.

And momentum is building. Awareness of the issues facing Black, other ethnic minority, LGBTQ+ and neurodiverse investment professionals is higher than ever, with networks and mentoring circles created and flourishing. Firms have come together to diversify their early careers recruitment via the Investment Industry Springboard, as well as supporting after-school clubs for disadvantaged and ethnically-diverse students. The cross-company Returners programme is attracting hundreds of applicants each year from those (mainly women) who have left the industry and are seeking to return. We are well on our way to reaching the goal of 1000 LGBTQ+ role-models and allies throughout the industry. And we've been sharing best practice and developing guidance for inclusive recruitment, smart working, line management, allyship and building back more equally post-COVID.

The pandemic has created both opportunities and threats for diversity and inclusion efforts but with our lives turned upside down and working practices changed overnight, there is now a bigger moment to seize. With the scale of participation and level of commitment, I feel more optimistic than ever that we can and will continue to make progress.

I'm incredibly grateful to Steve Butler for taking the time to compile this book to showcase the Diversity Project's efforts to date. You'll read the personal stories of many of the leaders involved in the Project, which bring the issues alive. Their practical suggestions will help you if you're considering either a similarly comprehensive project or narrower efforts to address specific areas of diversity. You'll get a sense of the breadth of the Project – we are tackling every dimension of diversity and at all career stages. You'll see that the actions are mounting up. This is a work-in-progress but a great lesson in how a group of people determined to make change are making it happen.

I hope you enjoy reading it and seeing how much more can be achieved over the next five years!

Best wishes, Helena

Contents

Chapter 1
Introduction

As an industry, the investment and savings industry is not representative of the population as a whole. In London, where the majority of fund managers are based, 18.5% of the population is Asian and 13.3% is black. Yet, in the fund management industry, 10% of individuals identify as Asian and only 1% identify as black.

While female employment rates across the board in the UK are not that far behind their male counterparts (72.4% in October - December 2019 compared with 80.6%[1]), the proportion of female fund managers in the UK has stubbornly hovered around 10% over the past four years - and just 4% of money managed is run exclusively by women.

That pay gap between men and women within fund management is actually the second largest of any sector in the UK, with only investment banking registering worse figures.

Despite all of the educational, demographic, social and cultural shifts we have witnessed in recent years, for anyone to rise to the top in the financial services sector it remains far more difficult if you do not come from a narrow band

---

[1] https://researchbriefings.files.parliament.uk/documents/SN06838/SN06838.pdf

of the population: white males, privately educated and from a select group of Universities.

Why does this matter?

Apart from the inequality of opportunity and unfairness this represents, it means that the sector is missing out on a huge talent pool, one that offers the life experiences and cognitive diversity that can tap more directly into the way other parts of the population live and think. That diversity of thinking can not only help businesses design new products and services which better meet the needs and ambitions of their clients; it also allows the industry as a whole to meet challenges in a way less hidebound by the "group think" that – arguably – led to the worst excesses of the last financial crisis.

Then we must look at the compelling fact that every business has to concern itself with where the next generation of talent is going to come from. In my 2019 book "Manage the Gap"[2], I set out some of the many ways in which younger people coming into businesses or rising through the ranks see the world very differently than previous generations.

They increasingly demand equality of opportunity - regardless of background, gender, ethnicity, disability, or

[2] Butler, S. 2019 Manage the Gap: Achieving Success with Intergenerational Teams, London: ReThink Press

orientation. They expect to be allowed to strike a work/life balance that allows them to have a family and a personal life. They want the company they work for to embody ideals and social purpose that align with their own. And, if the employer they are with can't deliver that, they will take their talents elsewhere.

If the investment and savings sector fails to woo today's graduates, where will tomorrow's leaders come from?

Investors and clients – who are increasingly global – also expect the people who manage their money to have socially fair work practices in place, and to reflect themselves and the world they live in. The days when investors were primarily white males from a wealthy background, comfortable with someone who echoed their own background to handle their business, are long gone.

The solution?

So, what is the investment and savings industry doing to ensure they keep pace with the progress we are seeing in the rest of society, and that the sector is fit for purpose for the future?

In early 2016, a group of leaders in the investment and savings profession recognised that future success for their clients, members, employers, and shareholders requires an inclusive culture and decided to take action to accelerate progress towards this.

That initiative led to the Diversity Project which has since made huge strides in raising awareness of the issues and galvanising support for their aims. However, as this book makes clear, there is still a long way to go.

By exploring the Diversity Project and offering practical ways forward, the purpose of this book is to provide helpful guidelines on how senior and middle managers, if they are genuinely intent on making their businesses more diverse and inclusive, can establish and foster a culture that will make sure that (like the lettering in a proverbial stick of rock) everyone within the company is on-board with the mission of being truly diverse and inclusive.

The book is based upon the vision of the Diversity Project, which was set up specifically to address the challenges I listed above and grounded on the powerful personal stories and experiences of some of those leading the various workstreams.

The Founders

The Diversity Project did not spring fully-formed out of the ground: it was forged by the experiences of a small group of people who were determined to make sure that life as part of a minority group would be easier for the next generation than it was for them. And while its roots were in gender diversity, it soon became something far wider-reaching. I asked Jane Welsh, Sarah Bates, Alexandra

Haggard, and Helena Morrissey what inspired them to found the Diversity Project. Here are their stories.

Sarah Bates

> "I still think we're not great at working out how different people can contribute to a group and tend to be rather conformist when recruiting new people, making it harder for some to break through. In part, and this is the bit that worries me, as we have tried to make the process more objective, we have given recruitment some systematic bias."

— Sarah Bates

I'm a Manchester girl. I went to State school – although it was a direct grant Grammar School – and then Cambridge. In 1980, when I graduated, there were very few jobs going. But it was just at the time when UK brokers were looking for research analysts. No one in my family had ever worked in anything to do with finance but it sounded interesting, and off I went.

I got a job as an analyst at a firm called Simon & Coates, at the time when Gavyn Davie was the Economist there. It was one of the early research-based firms, and guess what they asked me to do? Food retailing. I moved over to fund management in 1982, to what was the National Provident Institution.

Interestingly, when I joined, there were no established career paths in the broking, savings, and investment business... it was rather more eccentric than that; less stratified. You didn't have to have read the city pages of whatever newspaper from the age of 12, have had work experience in lots of grand firms, or have joined the City Club at University. So, arguably, in some ways, it was more open to certain groups than it later became.

The Mercer survey[3], which looked at diversity within the industry by gender and other groups, at the beginning of the Diversity Project, rather demonstrated that narrowing of the sector over the years.

There were some pretty senior women fund managers around the place when I started at the NPI. Better than it is now. That said, women seemed to be asked to do things that were perhaps seen as less mainstream: we had a woman in charge of the American desk, and another in charge of the Japanese desk. The blokes were in charge of the UK!

I went to a predecessor company of Invesco as a fund manager, then became head of UK equities, before a brief spell

---

[3] https://diversityproject.com/resource/diversity-projectmercer-benchmarking-study

as COO. After I'd had our daughter in 1993, I ran the investment trusts and other specialist divisions and then became CEO of the institutional business in the UK.

I only took three months maternity leave - at that point there was nothing but statutory maternity pay (about £90 a week for six weeks) to fall back on, so choices were somewhat limited. But at the time it didn't seem that odd. My mother worked as a medical secretary at Wythenshawe Hospital and was quite a radical. I didn't realise that that was an unusual background until much later – in fact, until I saw my own contemporaries bringing up their own kids.

There have been some interesting ebbs and flows in all this. Having parents who were children of the 60s, women's lib was regarded as pretty mainstream for my generation... the generations that came later saw some backward steps I think – especially around social mobility. If you were born in 1958, your father's income had little correlation with your own income. It wasn't like that if you were born in 1978.

A gay friend once told me that when homosexuality was illegal, the groupings were pretty unstratified. When people came out more into the open, you went back to the usual class system. And I think there are some interesting analogies elsewhere.

If you listen to Gavin Lewis, he would say that the experience of being Black British – and in his case, coming from Tottenham – is radically different from the experience of being part of the middle class West African diaspora.

Have I met with sexism along the way? I remember my first boss telling me soon after I started that "You'll have to be a bit less girly". I've never been particularly girly. I just think he was trying to express something… God knows what it was. I've run across that time after time, including at the board of a fairly major company, when the outgoing chairman said: "We interviewed another one of you…"

I didn't realise what he meant until about 24 or 48 hours later.

In my first few jobs, people would say to me: "Oh, you have to be much better to get anywhere if you're a woman."

People also talk about tokenism. I've been appointed to chair 11 different organisations – from charities and not-for-profits to investment trust boards and a FTSE 100 company – and seven of those were from having been a board member. So, I have to assume that was on merit rather than tokenism.

I still think we're not great at working out how different people can contribute to a group and tend to be rather conformist when recruiting new people, making it harder for some to break through. Partly it's because financial services ARE now seen as a career, so lots of people apply. In part, and this is the bit that worries me, as we have tried to make the process more objective, we have given recruitment some systematic bias.

How did you get involved with the Diversity Project?

I was chair of the investment panel at St Joseph's Hospice and sitting at some fund manager's entertainment do and this chap from a big firm told me that only 13% of their graduate applicants were female. That comment started me off on my particular journey.

I asked why, and he said it was because they recruit largely mathematicians and then put them through a bear pit recruitment process. And I thought, well that's not really a starter, is it? A, it's pretty culturally biased. B, there ARE women mathematicians, and C, if you're putting people off by your recruitment processes, isn't there something wrong with them?

So, I checked that stat out with a couple of fund managers at big fund management firms and they too came up with 13 to 14%. Some firms do better, but that's still worse than when I started.

I really hate the intern systems where friends of Mummy and Daddy get you jobs – that's really dysfunctional. We are trying to be objective, trying to be fair, but we've ended up with processes that defeat part of their objective. We have a belief that we are picking the best people with a rather dodgy definition of what "best" actually means.

For example, we know that if, in the job spec or advertisement, we use language in certain ways, we put off women and probably other groups too. If, perhaps, you are introverted, have a sense of self-doubt and don't think you walk on water, are you really going to apply for some of these careers?

All these people who say, "We want the best person for the job" are not thinking things through. What you really want is the person who is going to make the group do better.

I remember asking Andy Hornby, who was at the helm at HBOS in 2008, who had contributed most on his board during the crash, and he said it was the people who had, hitherto, been the most difficult. They were the ones who responded most rapidly and most objectively to changing facts. It wasn't the people who had been the most collegiate.

After that, I spent some time trying to recruit people who were more disruptive to the boards I was involved with and I have learned that it's important that disruptors understand how to influence as well. There's a fine line between being disruptive and destructive.

So, the conversation at that dinner started me down this road. I got Jane and Alexandra together for lunch and we had a collective rant. Jane and I go back a long way – she and I are good examples of cognitive diversity. She is incredibly bright and thinks things through very clearly and patiently, and I go off at tangents. And that combination can work quite well, I think.

I was interested in the extraordinary stats: why has this gone backwards? Alexandra got the bit between her teeth and rang up Helena. We got together and Helena came up with this structure which doesn't have a command and control: as we would be relying on volunteers, it wasn't going to happen otherwise.

We set up the workstreams and some of them took off immediately because of the combined passion of a small group of people; some didn't or took more time. But overall, it has worked because of its flexible structure – and that was Helena's great gift.

I think that some of what is going on as a result of the pandemic will make a profound difference towards enabling greater diversity and inclusion in the workplace – working from home, for instance, which is profoundly different from what people have been telling us over the last 15 or

20 years. That should make a huge difference to people who are disabled, and those with more complicated lives for whatever reason.

However, I do think there is a danger that, in times of crisis, people tend to hunker down and go back to their own tribes. People will say we can't be doing things that are seen as luxuries, and some bits of diversity can be seen as that.

Another thing that's happened in this crisis is that the benefits of different sorts of resilience are becoming quite obvious and having to cope with the current situation may make people more aware of the benefits of cognitive diversity. In FCA terms, it's a sandbox.

It may also change some behaviours. I had a wonderful conversation recently with someone whose boss is a bit shouty, and she said that this was OK when it's at work, "but when he's shouting into my bedroom via Zoom – it's in my home".

So how can we instil greater diversity and inclusion in our businesses?

It's about thinking through, as hard as you can, what characteristics are going to make your team work better.

And what would success in ten years' time look like for the Diversity Project?

We wouldn't have to exist.

Jane Welsh

"The end benefit to companies is cognitive diversity within the business: there are lots of ways to define it, but basically, it's people who think differently.... perhaps the big picture, perhaps the small detail. The evidence suggests that if you have a group of people who all think alike, even if they are very smart, they are going to miss things."

— Jane Welsh

I began life in Yorkshire and started my career straight out of University, marketing early versions of portfolio risk analysis to asset managers and owners. I was, looking back, something of an oddity: a young woman in a world that was predominantly male and a lot older than me. And they definitely had different accents to mine!

When I moved to Frank Russell Company, I set up their first manager research capability in the UK and also began an MBA at around the same time. I was always interested in group dynamics, and what makes a good team. I was quite taken with the concept of "groupthink" and observing teams that seemed to spar off each other: people who brought different things to the table versus teams that looked like clones. I was looking for evidence of internal challenge within investment teams.

My work with trustee boards also helped me understand how it feels to be the outsider. And, again, when I went to Willis Towers Watsons, I moved into the world of actuaries where I was definitely the outsider within a monoculture: mostly men; all mathematicians; all very smart.

Around 2011 or 2012, my interest in diversity led to me chairing the company's inclusion and diversity council, which was looking at how we attract, retain, develop, and promote diverse talents... and specifically how we gave opportunities to some people but not to others.

In December 2015, I was having lunch with Sarah Bates and Alexandra Haggard and got onto the topic of "where have all the women gone". When we started out in our careers, although the industry was tiny compared to now, there was a higher proportion of women around than there is now. We wondered why that might be.

That led to a second observation: if we started out today, would we even get a job in the industry? Both because of the way that big firms recruit at graduate level, focussing on particular universities and people with particular subject backgrounds, but also, self-selection by students as well. There is a perception that, unless you're studying maths, finance or economics, you wouldn't consider a career in this industry. And unless your mum or dad, uncle or aunt, worked in this industry, you wouldn't even know about it.

If only a narrow range of people was bothering to apply, we worried about the potential narrowing of cognitive diversity.

But we put aside the gloomier thoughts (perhaps the wine was starting to cut in) and had a more positive thought: despite these concerns, we all knew individual firms doing some really good work around D&I. If we shared what worked and what doesn't, we could speed up the progress of the whole industry.

That was the idea that led to The Diversity Project. But who could kick-start it? The obvious answer was Helena, who was then chairing the Investment Association, had started the 30% club and was passionate about diversity. If anyone could help get this idea off the ground, it would be her...

Right from the initial conversation, we were looking to include other groups as well as gender... ethnicity and LGBT were included very early on, and, every now and then, a new area gets added, because people are passionate about that dimension, and there are enough people to pursue it.

The transition from that first conversation with Helena to where it is today is just incredible.

We're a very "bottom-up" organisation, and it's worked by finding someone who is very passionate about a particular issue and helping them find friends who are similarly passionate and letting them get on with it. I hope that people feel like we are a supportive umbrella!

In Summer 2016, we had a "soft launch" and invited the CEOs of organisations that we knew from across the industry. About 30 turned up, and there was so much support for what we were trying to do; ideas and input as well as pledges in terms of financial support. And that gave us the confidence to keep going with it.

"Let's not boil the ocean" was another guiding principle. We deliberately focussed on investment and savings – a sector we understood and could manage. We knew who all the right people were to get involved. And we knew there was a real problem that needed to be addressed.

If we look at the gender pay gap as a measure of the challenge, it is the second-highest of any sector. And it is a very traditional industry – there are lots of good reasons for that but that doesn't mean that change isn't needed. It's also a very low turnover industry: people stay in their jobs as portfolio and asset managers, or as consultants in consulting firms, for a very long time.

One of the first things we did was conduct a survey, which Mercer ran for us[4], to get a grip on the scale of the challenge. Some 24 asset management firms took part and nearly 4,000 individuals. The results confirmed what we already knew: the dominance of men in the asset management/portfolio management function, the high degree of private education in the industry relative to society as a whole, the low number of Black employees, and the low number of people who would describe themselves as disabled, relative to the working population as a whole.

A few years on, we still have a huge distance to go – we certainly haven't shifted the dial yet. What we're pushing for is culture change if we're to create more inclusive organisations, and that obviously has to come from the top. But we're also targeting some of our efforts at how we can support line managers, who are key to this. They're doing what they've been told to do – focus on output – and they haven't always been supported to spend time creating an inclusive culture.

---

[4]https://diversityproject.com/resource/diversity-projectmercer-benchmarking-study

The end benefit to companies is cognitive diversity within the business. There are lots of ways to define this, but basically, it's people who think differently.... perhaps the big picture, perhaps the small detail. The evidence suggests that if you have a group of people who all think alike, even if they are very smart, they are going to miss things.

If you have a group of people who look at the world differently, and if people listen to those different viewpoints, which is always the challenge, there's a chance that they might pick up some of those risks or opportunities.

How can businesses start to address this? Start with the data, because a lot of companies are in denial. They may have gender data but often very little else. And it's not just about staff numbers: then you can see what your retention rates are like for each category and how each progresses. And then it's a matter of making this part of their business strategy, seeing this as who they are as an organisation and what they want to be going forwards.

It can't just be a nice little thing that they add on at the end. It's got to come from the top. A lot of leaders do get this – but they have got to live and breathe it, and make sure that the everyday experience aligns with that. Many companies say they do D&I... but staff are still expected to make calls at four in the morning.

I remember talking to one lady a couple of years ago who worked for one of the big investment banks. They spent a vast amount on D&I and they'd recruited her because she had a slightly different background. When she joined, she told them she had other commitments outside work, and they said that's brilliant, that's why we hired you.

The first weekend she had to work all weekend. She told them that this hadn't been part of the deal, and they said it wouldn't happen again. But the same thing happened the next weekend. And the next. Eventually, she left.

So how can we instil greater diversity and inclusion in our businesses?

It's the everyday behaviours that have to change, not the big statements and the policies.

Alexandra Haggard

"We have to take advantage of this opportunity and maximise the potential for change. Let's not lose the moment."

— **Alexandra Haggard**

I started as an intern at Russell Investments (or Frank Russell Company as it was then) in 2002. I was very fortunate with a series of super managers who helped me progress rapidly through the ranks. In August 2008, I was promoted to running the product development and product management team.

At that point, I had an awakening. I found myself regularly in the room with the executive committee, and they had a certain number of things in common. They were all male, at least 10 years older than I was... and had wives who didn't work. They were all wonderful people – and some are lifelong friends. But I was very different from them.

The biggest impact of this difference was that I couldn't get my voice heard. I happened, at the time, to meet the most extraordinary woman: Anna Ostergren, an acting coach and theatre director. Working with her has been really influential in my life: like Margaret Thatcher (though it sounds rather grand comparing myself!), I learnt to use my voice and body differently so that I would actually be seen and heard in these meetings. Gradually, I started to find ways to communicate more effectively, which, along with some good old-fashioned hard work, helped me continue to grow and learn at Russell for another six years. I'm lucky that what it took me was an investment in acting coaching – unfortunately, it would still take something more revolutionary for others to be heard in our meeting rooms.

In 2013, I was headhunted to be the CEO of Stamford Associates: a small investment consulting firm with incredible connections - including Helena. I've been very fortunate that Sarah Bates has been my mentor since 2008. She and I had been debating what to do about the diversity challenge. She introduced me to her great friend, Jane Welsh and the three of us got together. We were inspired by the 30% Club and wanted to bring it to asset management. The change was that we wanted to look at all aspects of diversity and wanted to think about the entire talent pipeline from student to NED. When we later discussed it with Helena, it was clear that she had been thinking something quite similar, so we had an instant meeting of the minds.

By the time Helena hosted our first meeting, we'd all been working in the background – we were already eight, and Helena had pulled in the Investment Association. It was clear that we were all prepared to make time to drive this idea forward.

From there, the project snowballed. We benefitted enormously from having Helena in the conversation because of her role in the industry. People were keen to be involved, and it was exciting.

The organisation has always been quite grassroots. There isn't a "top-down, this is where we're going, and this is how we're going to do it" approach. If you've got a good idea, you use the project as an umbrella and get on with it.

One of my significant contributions early on was to introduce Linda Russheim to the group. She has run the marketing strategy for the Project since the beginning, and her selfless — and brilliant — contribution to communications and marketing has been one of the biggest dial movers in terms of really getting the message out.

I've played a number of different roles, depending upon what was needed and what I could give at any time. I'm leading the Disability workstream now and enjoying the opportunity we have to drive change in an area that still needs so much more work. I feel an enormous amount of pride for what has been achieved. We've helped to amplify the conversation and take advantage of some very difficult moments in society, capitalise upon them and find a way to make them more positive and turn them into change.

Gavin Lewis, for instance, and the messaging he's created around "Talk About Black", has really stepped up the conversation around racial inclusion, particularly in this last very difficult year.

Where do we need to go from here?

We need more women, we need more black people, we need more people in the industry who are disabled, and so many other cognitively diverse people. There's still masses to do, but I think we're having much better conversations. And I think they are being had in different places.

We have to be really focussed on making sure that it's actions, not words. But now is when we have the opportunity for the most change because it is unquestionably an inflection point in society.

If you had asked people in January whether they could have their entire workforce work from home, you would have been laughed out of the room. If you'd asked whether people would be as focussed on racial equity this year, I doubt they would have said yes. We have to take advantage of this opportunity and maximise the potential for change. Let's not lose the moment.

"It's still really hard to move the needle: we have fabulous grassroots support and some great leaders; it's the bit in the middle that's still a problem. The investment industry generally has been slow on D&I, and a little arrogant – which is a bit ironic when they themselves pressure companies on these issues."

— **Helena Morrissey**

Setting up the 30% Club introduced the idea of pressing the case for more women at a senior level, but it was only at board level and it was only women. And while I had been involved in setting up a women's network inside my own firm, I hadn't felt able to go beyond that and look at diversity in the round. When I became Chair of the Investment Association in 2014, I think a lot of people expected me to focus almost entirely on diversity – but the industry faced a lot of other challenges as well. It wasn't until 2016 when Alexandra Haggard, Jane Welsh and Sarah Bates came to see me and I felt that – yes, now was the time. They are all wonderful successes in their own parts of the industry, and all were genuinely concerned we were going backwards when it came to diversity and inclusion. I was staying on for an extra year as Chair at the IA: establishing an initiative to start moving us forwards again became a pressing goal for my final year.

Before the 2007/8 crisis, it was hard to make a case on business grounds for having more women. There was talk about equal opportunities, diversity and inclusion networks and affinity groups, that sort of thing, but I always thought it made no sense to only have people from a very narrow educational background as well as the same gender, same geography, same social class, friends with each other... it's very difficult for them to challenge each other. It's not human nature. Part of their identity is the group they associate with, and we're not programmed to undermine our own group.

I saw first-hand the trajectory of the RBS going into the crash, because Newton ran the pension fund and I ran all the fixed income part of that. And over the 10 or so years prior to that, we had meetings in Edinburgh and saw their evolution from a group of very mild, modest Scottish people to a situation where they were talking about installing helipads.

At the last dinner we had with them, my colleagues and I came out of that room and said: "My God..." It was quite plain to see how they had gone into this bubble where they could do no wrong.

I've always thought that if we have more diverse thinking around the table, we're more likely to come up with solutions to some of the problems that we face. In the aftermath of the financial crisis, people were talking about groupthink, and the regulators, in their report, cited lack of challenge in the downfall of RBS, as well as Fred Goodwin's dominating style. On the board were 17 men and one woman, and most of the men were from Edinburgh. A few months before the crash, they appointed an Englishman to the board, and this was trumpeted as a great example of diversity. They hung out together; many had been to the same school together.

It's still really hard to move the needle: we have fabulous grassroots support and some great leaders; it's the bit in the middle that's still a problem. The investment industry generally has been slow on D&I, and a little arrogant — which is a bit ironic when they themselves pressure companies on these issues. If you just look at gender, Citywire has done their Alpha Female report for four years, and in that time, we've crept up from 10.2% of fund managers being women to 10.8%.

We're saying the fund management industry isn't diverse in any dimension: socio-economical, ethnicity, disability, gender, and so forth. It's diversity across the piece. Now we have a sense of urgency about it, and we're looking at every stage of the career, every aspect of the problem. I am confident that we will get some breakthroughs in underlying areas.

Sadly, there is no silver bullet, but I think one of the problems generally for the industry is that it's not well known – people don't know someone who works in it – so we have to go out more and be in schools and universities, team up with other people in the city and create a programme to give them work experience before University.

Relative to any stage in our past, there is genuine desire for change at the very top. But diversity still wouldn't, for instance, be a regular item on the agenda in strategy meetings or board discussions. For some Chairmen and CEOs, diversity is something for when you've got spare time and there are no other crises to deal with.

I've been hard at work on some of these issues for 15 years. There's always something, a reason to prioritise something else – a currency crisis, Brexit, an election, coronavirus. But if we'd never bothered, we'd still be stuck in the Dark Ages. We have to be careful about pushing it too hard in one sense because there are a lot of hurdles to get over and we need sustained energy and commitment – it's easy for people to feel they've 'been there, done that' when there's still so much to do.

What would you see as success for the Diversity Project?

Naively, I thought we'd get some signs of change in the first five years, but that's unlikely. So, in the next 5-10 years, success would be having colleagues as diverse as the population. We have some specific goals around some of the underlying diversity dimensions - 30% of female fund managers, 1,000 out and openly gay people in the industry – and I think we'll get there well before that. Having identified 15 black fund managers, we'll look for a meaningful target on that.

But it really is being an industry that is vibrant, futureproof, looks and feels very different... and you wouldn't know it from a company in another sector.

Part of achieving those objectives will mean more people stepping up as mentors. Everyone who has made it to any level in our industry has had some sort of ally or mentor along the way. No one is an island, and, if you're not powerful, you ideally need someone who is more powerful to be your mentor.

We have to not just redouble our existing efforts but refine them. And we'll be refreshing the messages – not just banging people over the head. They have to see that it's what they want – not just what they're expected or pressured to do. If you went into any senior group in an investment company before lockdown, it would have looked different from 10 years ago.

But it is still only baby steps. We need a big "whoosh" so you don't even think about diversity any more.

Chapter 2
Gender Equality

"The gender equality workstream involves men and women determined to level the playing field for women in the investment and savings industry, so they can achieve their full potential and contribute to a better, more inclusive culture."

— Helena Morrissey

Currently, gender pay gaps in asset management are the second-largest of any UK sector, while approximately 10% of fund managers are currently female. Just 4% of money managed in the UK is run exclusively by women.

Yet the fight for gender equality has been going on now for decades, so progress has been glacially slow – leading to a recent "re-set" of the Diversity Project's workstream's aims and targets. Is the problem one of recruitment... development... an inability amongst firms to accommodate career breaks? Baroness Helena Morrissey DBE has been in the vanguard of tackling this issue within the sector and beyond for many years. Here is her take.

Helena Morrissey

When I joined Schroders back in 1987, the month of the Crash, they sent me out straight from a Graduate programme to New York. My experiences there were pretty favourable: there were four people around the office, two men who ran the money and two women who ran the business, and the women seemed to call most of the shots – to my naïve eyes anyway! They were certainly very highly regarded and very much in control of their own destiny.

In hindsight, they were also great role models for me... but what I didn't appreciate at the time was how unusual it was to have that gender balance.

I came back to London after two years to find myself the only woman in the team and immediately recognised that the situation in New York had been quite anomalous.

I then got married and, within a year, had my first child. That exposed me rather abruptly to gender issues within the industry. This was the era when people talked openly in the office about going to lap dancing clubs with clients. There was a lot of banter, and I'd wince and try to hide away.

When I came back from maternity leave and had my first conversation with my boss, I was eligible for my first promotion from graduate trainee to manager. I didn't get it while all my male peers did. I asked what I was doing wrong and was told, "Your performance is great. But there's some doubt about your commitment because of you having a baby."

I'd only taken five months off. I'd kept up with developments… having investment papers dropped through my letterbox every week. I wasn't showing any sign of being less committed. I remember challenging him and being told that his boss – also obviously a man – was "quite old-fashioned" about these things.

It was a rude awakening. Until then, probably naïvely, I'd never thought it could have any impact on my career. I realised that I had to make a decision: to put up, shut up or move on.

I didn't move immediately because I had a small child and a lot of things going on, but I started looking around and was headhunted about a year later to join Newton Investment Management, which was quite different… not least because my boss was a woman.

The founder, Stewart Newton, interviewed me and told me that they had a special maternity policy that provided about six months' full pay then helped you to return to work. They were very proactive about being family-friendly, and also welcomed diversity of thought. After I was appointed, Stewart mentored me, and I remember him saying: "Don't ever hide the fact that you're a mother. Or be embarrassed about any of the things you need to do around that. That's part of your perspective. It's what brings you to this firm and what makes you different."

He had built the whole firm around this philosophy that diversity of thought (although he called it "multiple perspectives" as no one then was using the word "diversity") would achieve the best investment results. In that, he was well ahead of his time.

I should add that Schroders did then have two very powerful women in the London office. The rest of the firm was very hierarchical, traditional, silver-trolleyed, butlers — stuff they would wince at now – but at the other end, there was this little club of women that was mutually supportive. In contrast, Newton had a culture of diversity running through it like the words in a stick of rock, although I didn't realise quite how unusual that was at the time.

It was said that you could always tell someone from firms like Goldman Sachs walking down the street because of their swagger! We, on the other hand, took pride in being something of a motley crew, and loved gathering people who had an interesting perspective. Everybody had a quirk. That said, everyone was polished enough and had a real passion for what they did.

Our strapline then was "no one has a monopoly on great ideas". The firm had a boutique feel and clients seemed to like having characterful people's approach to money.

As I developed my career at Newton, I was put in charge of global bond funds – running them in what would now be regarded in a rather swashbuckling way, with big positions in both duration and currency. The competition weren't just all men...but seemingly, all men called Paul, so I stood out a bit. Having formerly regarded being a woman as something of an albatross round my neck, I realised it could also be an advantage. I was winning awards - although I wasn't always sure if it was just because I was the one that judges could pick out on a line up parade.

Looking back, the culture was key. Having failed at the first hurdle in my first job, I became CEO at 35 with five children, seven years after joining and that was all down to the cultural differences.

It was very meritocratic, and if you wanted responsibility, you'd be given it. My boss left after my first year while I was on maternity leave. I came back a bit earlier than anticipated and asked Stewart if I could look after the funds until they found a replacement. He said: "Sure, but you'll have to sit next to me, and at 5 pm every day, tell me what you've been up to."

After about a year, once he was comfortable, he took the stabilisers off.

But even when I became chief executive, I felt I had to earn that job: I had the title but not the mandate, so I focused entirely on winning credibility in the role and didn't do anything around diversity or gender at first. We were also on the sell list at the time I became CEO so it was probably a full four or five years, while we steadied the ship, before I started thinking about what I could do to make it easier for women coming up behind me.

Around 2005, 'Diversity' was starting to be bandied about a bit. I was feeling a lot more confident and Newton were back on the buy list. I was asked to join the board of the Investment Association as their first female director - and that was an eye-opener. I'd be chatting to the other board members and realised that they'd gone to prep school together forty years before!

There was no desire to change anything within the industry. Everybody was quite comfortable with their lot. Within my own firm, I discussed starting a woman's development network - I became the co-chair of Mellon International, Newton's parent company, so I used that as a platform to get something going inside the firm. I focused on the women in Newton and across the rest of Mellon in EMEA, and we ran lots of events and workshops around career development.

But my efforts weren't entirely successful. It was tending to be women talking to women about women's issues. Men were still very much a minority. We lacked clear-cut measurable targets, so there was no way of knowing if we were getting anywhere.

And then came the financial crisis, so no one could exactly claim things were perfect. That's when I started to talk to women outside the industry: I got a group together of about 40 women and we agreed that we were making very little progress in senior roles and on boards.

Most of the women were very sceptical about possible progress. They certainly wanted it to happen, but they felt worn down by their experiences. The most typical reaction was "We won't be able to change anything".

The genesis of the 30% Club is well-documented. I was invited to speak on diversity and inclusion at a lunch at Goldman Sachs – there was a mix of men and women from different sectors – and we discussed how difficult it was to make much progress beyond around 10% women at senior levels. That's when I had a lightbulb moment: I came away thinking it doesn't make any sense. We've got ready, able and willing women feeling frustrated with the situation and companies that want them to progress.

What are we doing wrong?

I started reading widely around organisational behaviours and how you achieve change. That's when I read about Deutsche Telekom trying to get 30% women on all levels - and for business reasons: to get the best talent, the best thinking. And I realised that in groups where women make up one third, you feel part of the group. Fewer than that and you can feel a bit token. That's where the 30% target came from.

By then, I'd left the IA board because I wasn't enjoying it, then in 2014, they invited me back to be Chair. People said you must start working on diversity within the industry now. I was a little reluctant to do that – not least because I was still quite new and one of only two women on the board. Again, I felt I had to earn the right to be in that position ahead of waving a diversity flag, and we had a lot of other problems to deal with. Maybe that's me, but I genuinely think that's something that a lot of women experience.

So, it wasn't until 2016 when Jane and Sarah came to see me, and I felt that – yes, now was the time. I was staying on for an extra year at the IA so that became an obvious thing to do with my last year. Now I head up the Gender workstream.

What is currently being achieved, and what more needs to be done?

Despite making some progress over the last five years, there is still so much more to do — which is why we "re-launched" in July 2020 with new targets which include a halving of the industry's gender pay gaps and a 30% female fund manager target by 2030. Citywire has done an Alpha Female report for four years and their data shows we've crept up from 10.2% fund managers around the world to 10.8% in that time — so there's a long way to go.

All the evidence suggests that we are making painfully slow progress towards encouraging more women into fund management and to build their careers in our industry. At the same time, a sense of fatigue has set in around the topic of gender diversity.

Yet the arguments for having more women run money, manage people, lead client relationships, and contribute to our industry's culture and future are stronger than ever. We have analysed the obstacles and devised a new intensive, wide-ranging set of initiatives to address them and create new enablers for women to progress.

Compared with the time when I joined the industry, I think it's probably more off-putting for women now joining because we were blissfully ignorant. When I was interviewed on the "milk round", men and women were applying, and interviews were with a man and woman panel. Diana Noble, who interviewed me, had a big influence on me.

I do think that behaviours generally are – I wouldn't say perfect – but more subtle now around the issues that women face. We might not get the banter I had to put up with, however, sometimes it's quite insidious. Women are led to believe they will be quite welcome, and that's true in many firms but sometimes poor behaviours – patronising talk or simply not being managed properly – still get in the way. I now see great commitment to resolve these issues though and that's exciting.

When I joined the industry, it felt that the only way to get on was by being an "honorary man". And that takes away from the whole point about diversity. Young women coming in – and there aren't enough of them – should feel confident that people are much more aware of this and the need to value people for what they bring to the table. Fund management is a fabulous career for anyone who wants to be measured on results. I know that ultimately enabled me to succeed; it wasn't about hours worked at the same desk; it was about making the right judgements.

What is the way forward, do you think?

We can also contribute something beyond our technical skills by being empathetic as well, building relationships.

Now we have a sense of urgency about it - no stone un-turned, every stage of the career, every aspect of the prob-lem. I think the investment industry generally has been slow on D&I, and a little bit arrogant – which is a bit ironic when they themselves pressure companies on these is-sues.

The pandemic has created a crossroads moment; many women have struggled both in our industry and of course more broadly in society as we've borne the brunt of child-care and other domestic duties, but we've also been able to demonstrate that we can all work productively from home. It's given a glimpse into how things could be more modern, more genuinely family-friendly.

We need to be very careful at this juncture. People are now talking about hybrid ways of working which will help men and women to lead more equal lives.

Firms can choose to make a conscious decision to ensure that women don't slide backwards. Ideally, we'll end up in a position where men, as well as women, can have real work life balance and that will enable more women to take advantage of career opportunities. We need to make a conscious decision to create that different working envi-ronment now.

So, what can you and your organisation do to play your part in reducing gender inequality?

- Start by tracking your diversity data – not just numbers but also roles, retention, and progression. What are the numbers telling you about recruitment, turnover, the distribution of performance ratings and the gender pay gap?

- Make sure your recruitment processes aren't holding women back – for instance, does your website portray a diverse workforce and are your job descriptions gender-neutral?

- Ensure all job postings emphasise smart working options.

- Don't ask about prior salary – why perpetuate any gender pay gap that might exist?

- Try to hire in clusters: that way, it's a lot easier to hire diverse talent.

- Insist on diverse shortlists and diverse interview panels.

- Employ structured interview processes and cognitive tests to ensure you collect objective and comparable data on candidates.

- Consider a returnship programme to attract and support those who have taken an extended career break.

- Appoint people who will add the most to the team through complementary skills and perspectives while avoiding tokenism.

- Ensure that succession or talent management processes consider diversity.
- Support mentoring and sponsorship for women.
- Provide additional support around career breaks. Mentoring pre / during / post-maternity leave, for example, can help women maintain career progression. Revisit smart working policies and practices.
- If you have a gender pay gap, have a plan for closing it, not least by encouraging salary transparency.
- Encourage business leaders to be role models.
- At meetings, techniques like turn-taking, active listening and requiring unanimity can ensure that diverse talent feels listened to and that the team benefits from diverse viewpoints. This is particularly important when working by video or conference call.
- Embed smart working throughout the business and encourage everyone to be as effective as they can be: it is ok for different people in a team to work in different ways – we all need different things at different stages of our career.

Chapter 3
Ethnicity

"I've been saying this for years, but now I'm saying it with even more certainty, that the world is changing, and what made something successful then won't make it successful in the future."

— **Gavin Lewis**

The challenges and issues

The UK is the world's second-largest savings market after the United States and employs 100,000 individuals. Yet, in terms of ethnicity, the industry remains markedly unrepresentative of the UK population and workforce. Ethnic minorities comprise 14% of the UK population, with 7.5% identifying as Asian and 3.3% as Black. In London, where the majority of fund managers are based, 18.5% of the population is Asian and 13.3% is Black.

Yet, in the fund management industry, 10% of individuals identify as Asian and just 1% identify as Black.

Why? There is no one simple answer and no single "magic bullet" solution. Members of the Ethnicity workstream apply the metaphor of "kinks in the hose" when you're trying to water the garden. You can un-kink the piece of hose you can see but, still, no water flows. That's because, further back, a long way back, there are more kinks. You need to go right back to the tap, unkinking the hose at each point in order to get the water flowing.

In ethnicity terms, this means that you might well introduce diversity and inclusion practices in the workplace, but social investment and access to education are critical too if the water is to flow in the first place. Quite simply, unless you get that part sorted, a large swathe of young people will never get the qualifications they need to reach the application stage.

One of the factors complicating the issue is that not all ethnic minorities struggle equally to make their mark in the finance sector, which has led to the workstream focusing – for the present at least – much of its attention on Black rather than Asian communities.

Moreover, it has to be accepted that there is only so much "movement on the dial" that the Diversity Project and its supporters can make on its own. That issue has come right into the spotlight during the writing of this book with the Black Lives Matter campaign powerfully making the case that racism is systemic, and that only root and branch shifts in culture, attitudes, public policies, education and an understanding of history will lead to the long-term changes needed.

So how much do long-standing, underlying attitudes impact upon the challenge that Black people face when trying to reach their full potential in British society?

In the view of the workstream co-leader, Gavin Lewis: "Part of the problem can be tracked back to cultural differences – some of which are deeply rooted in history. In Britain, any conversation about slavery, and the part that Britain played in the slave trade, has routinely been quickly closed down. Because it happened 200 years ago, it isn't supposed to have any bearing on where we are now, so why do we even talk about it?"

"Thankfully, one of the positives that has come out of the tragic death of George Floyd, and the subsequent leap in public awareness of the Black Lives Matter Campaign, has been that slavery and its continuing grip on the relationship between black people and the rest of society has been the opening up of the discussion – even if the two sides of the debate seem even more divided than before."

"The toppling of one statue of a slave trader in Bristol has led to similar actions right around the world."

"My perspective? I know it's a thorny subject, however, it does have a bearing because you're talking about four hundred years of displacement of a people, placing them in a situation where they are powerless, economically enslaved – and I don't think that situation has changed."

"After migrants arrived in the UK, we still didn't have enough aspiration – not least because we'd been made to feel than it wasn't our place to aspire. And so, when black people have got into our industry, they feel that they have little or no chance of getting up the ladder… not helped by the fact that there aren't any black role models above them."

"It's a vicious circle: we don't aspire to reach the top, and the people who are at the top think you should be happy with what you've got."

Gavin Lewis

Ethnicity Workstream Leader

"I still often feel like a guest in the industry, and this has also been borne out by my peers… so I feel I have to watch what I say, how I say it, what I ask for, how I have discussions, my demeanour… Why?"

— Gavin Lewis

I grew up on council estates in Tottenham with my mum and my sister; and, as a black male growing up in Tottenham, the two main routes out were sport and music.

It was a very Alpha Male culture… a lot of violence and fighting… and until you come out of that and see the way other people live, you don't realise that this is not normal. Being so tall and gangly, I stood out like a sore thumb. I was always getting into fights.

I never really fitted in where I grew up, but I was good at two things. One was studying, the other was sports... and, luckily, sports let me hide the fact that I was a bit of a geek!

After experiencing some difficult situations, I decided quite early on that perhaps I could change my fortune and knuckled down to studying. I was fortunate to have a really strong mother who set an example. I saw her working late at night as a nurse, as well as studying to get into university, and that made a big impact on me.

So I studied. I got good grades in GCSEs and A levels and went to a good university, which took me out of my situation. But then I had no examples to follow in terms of the next stage. I thought that getting a good grade would be enough. I didn't realise that there was this whole other world of networking, sponsorship, work experience... and your face fitting.

There are many more Black graduates now who go to good universities and who are getting into the workplace: when I did that 20 years ago, I was a real anomaly. There was no guidance, no mentorship programmes, or someone like me who speaks out on this stuff.

Just getting through the door was a problem. I had the grades, but I was told I wasn't "rounded" like the other candidates. In their breaks from Uni, they'd been building wells in Africa or doing the Duke of Edinburgh's Award. I'd been stacking shelves in Sainsbury's. But I did get told that I was "really bright and articulate". Why "articulate" I've no idea... and I still hear that now.

How did you get where you are today?

After a few months, I decided to go into recruitment – not least because there appeared to be a lot of money to be made, and money was a big driver for me. I was working with asset managers and hedge fund managers and thought "I could do that job"; so, I basically used my recruitment skills on myself for about six months, trying to get a break into the industry.

Eventually, a start-up firm took me on. Initially, it was a three-month contract – a way in that turned into a permanent role. But it was in 2007, and what we didn't foresee was the financial Armageddon in 2008; there were times when I didn't even get paid. That was difficult but I felt I had to stay in order to get a role with a bigger asset manager.

When I was recruiting, one of my clients had been Russell Investments, and we'd kept in contact. I joined them for a few years as an institutional salesperson and then went to

UBS, where I was promoted to Executive Director, then got approached by Vanguard, and on to BlackRock where I've been since 2019.

I still often feel like a guest in the industry, and this has also been borne out by my peers... so I feel I have to watch what I say, how I say it, what I ask for, how I have discussions, my demeanour... Why? It's been a fight to get myself here, and there's almost a feeling that people are running a risk by taking me on, so that's left me – and others who've gone down the same road – somehow feeling we should be "indebted" or "grateful".

Why did I get involved with the Diversity Project? Because I've always been a minority in the industry, breaking new ground – but never really belonging or fitting in; an "out-sider", seeing everything like an observer. I know it's not right, but you get used to it – and I felt like I could be a role model, setting an example just by being in the industry.

At first, I was a bit sceptical about the Project: here's a bunch of middle-class white women... what do they know of my situation? Which shows you my own biases! But they've been the most supportive and inspirational group of people I've ever had the fortune to meet and work with. And the project has given us a real platform to voice our views on this issue.

Is the workstream making progress?

That depends on which day you catch me on!

On days when I'm drained from trying to do all of this, I can say to my wife, "I'm not sure that people really care about this," and Diversity becomes a tick box. But there are examples of where people have taken this personally and real change has happened.

Some days, I feel like D&I doesn't work for minority groups – for ethnic minorities in particular. Women still have a long way to go, but I think they can point to progress – although it's a very long time since the suffragettes first tied themselves to the railings!

It works for women because the door wasn't flung open for them by men. They forced it open for themselves. They were enough of them to push against the door, and they also know how the corporate world works... they were familiar faces to the white male majority. Also, they had economic influence, the ability to set up pressure groups and get support.

If you look at where ethnic minorities are, we don't have any of that. There's just a handful of us. Very few of us went to a private school. And we're not familiar. I feel like I'm a guest at times, like I have to wear a mask.

On other days, I'm overwhelmed by how many people get in touch, inspired, saying it's amazing what you've done, keep on. So that's progress. And the fact that this book has been written shows it's on the agenda.

What are the benefits, and the challenges, of ethnic diversity?

I still think we have a long way to go in the industry but for people like me, it's a good time to be at the level I'm at. I've been saying this for years, but now I'm saying it with even more certainty, that the world is changing, and what made something successful then won't make it successful in the future. You need people with different viewpoints, different perspectives, different life experiences. And ultimately, the world will hold us to account for society, our communities, and the planet.

The circumstances now will mean that maybe people like me will be able to play a bigger role.

I'm not someone who is keen on the "BAME" tag which groups everyone together. It's clearly an HR term to describe a group of people they don't know how to describe otherwise. For myself, I use the word "Black". I'm a Black person. And the diversity issue within the investment needs to be dissected because some groups have done far better than others in gaining senior roles within the industry. Indians have done well, but Bangladeshis and

Pakistanis less so. Black Africans have done better than West Indians.

There are a number of reasons for all of that, not least the aspirations that some communities have for their young people, and we are focusing on those groups that need the most help.

I think I've been fortunate in my career because I've had sponsors who have really invested in me. But I also think that's because I'm a bit of an outlier. I've got to the position where I know what I'm doing in my job. I'm providing leadership. I look at these initiatives to improve gender and they are fantastic, because women need the investment. But I'm looking at them as a black guy and thinking: "Wouldn't it be great for us to have something like this?"

Where it can become challenging is when diversity fatigue sets in and people start to think, "OK, we've let the women in, now here come the gays. Now bringing up the rear, oh God, look, there's some black people. We're full!"

That's my concern.

What needs to happen next?

Diversity solves one problem because it's preparing the workplace to get the best out of people who maybe don't fit the mould. The problem is that when you think about ethnicity and socio-economic stats, you have all these structural barriers that have been built up over years and years.

So, diversity is just one leg of the stool. Access to education and social investment are the others. And all three legs of the stool need to be in place. You can go to a good school, but if, when you get home in the evening, you're looking after your brothers because your mum's working two shifts, you won't have time to do your homework.

We need to invest in those poorer areas and improve their economic fortunes. I've given a lot of thought to it and I can't believe that the finance industry can't figure out ways to reduce inequality through what it invests in.

What can the investment and savings industry do in order to attract, progress and retain Black talent?

Here is the workstream's four-step action plan.

1. Pipeline
The challenge: UK Black-Caribbean and Black-African individuals experience higher rates of unemployment and are more likely to become victims of crime.

The solution: The creation of an after-school programme aimed at secondary school children which will help to equip them with the knowledge, tools, connections and, more importantly, aspiration to enter the fund management industry. A pilot programme is currently being planned with the City of London Corporation, initially working with one school in Tower Hamlets or Southwark and targeting children aged 11.

2. Entry

The challenge: Even when individuals achieve a good education, they are less likely to be successful in securing their preferred roles; they are either not attracted to asset management due to its perceived lack of diversity, or, in many cases, simply not aware.

The solution: An annual student event to identify and attract promising minority talent to the industry.

3. Progression

The challenge: When these Black individuals do break into the industry, they typically end up in support functions, have higher rates of attrition and rarely progress to leadership or revenue-generating positions. At the time of this book going to press, there are thirteen Black portfolio managers, three heads of distribution and only two Black professionals in C-Suite positions.

The solution:

- Mentoring circles led by senior ethnic minority professionals aimed at minority professionals with 1-10 years' experience.

- A proposed 5-point CEO plan which will equip business leaders with a blueprint to increase Black talent within their organisations.

4. Breaking the taboo

The challenge: Finally, whereas people are generally comfortable discussing issues relating to gender and, more increasingly, sexual orientation, race remains a taboo subject.

The solution: #talkaboutblack utilises thought leadership, roundtable debates, panel discussions, online videos, mainstream/trade media and social media to break the taboo subject that is race in our industry and society.

Here are ten actions you can take

If ten is too many, just choose one. But, choose one.

1. Have discussions with Black stakeholder groups. Ask how you can get involved. You'll find plenty, once you start to look.

2. Invite Black school kids to come to visit your offices for one day every quarter. Teach them essential skills for a day. Ask your staff to sign up for the programme and prepare to be inundated with volunteers.

3. Go to their schools and tell them they can be somebody; that you would love to help make it happen. Explain to the school head that you have a

special programme and that you're inviting 20 pupils to come to your headquarters once a quarter.

4. Actively pursue and recruit people of colour from universities you wouldn't normally consider; you'll be amazed at the talent, grit and diverse thinking you find. Send your CEO in person to give an inspirational talk to the university's Afro-Caribbean Society about values, purpose, and aspiration. Tell the students that if they graduate with a good degree, there's a place for them in your firm. Look them in the eye. Make them know you're serious. They will know that anyway because you're there in person.

5. Get tickets to see the next Chineke! Orchestra concert and take your team.

6. Take an interest in the lives and journeys of the Black people in your organisation. Take them out for coffee or lunch and ask to hear their stories. You'll be inspired. Maybe, you'll even appoint them to the C-Suite.

7. Put this specific issue onto your board agenda alongside the gender and LGBT items. It will force you to think deeply about it.

8. Set some measurable actions to commit to over the next year.

9. Ask five senior people in your firm (preferably those with absolutely no spare time) to commit to mentoring some of your more junior Black folk through the kinks.

10. Tell your firm you care about this issue, that you're committed to helping bring about change and that you want to see more Black people coming up through the firm. Ask for volunteers to help you think through what you can do.

Chapter 4
Age Diversity

Early Careers

"Our aim is to identify young people early on in their University careers – ideally their first year – gain their interest and broaden their knowledge of the sector, provide mentoring and support with getting internships and interviews, giving them the tools they need to be taken on by companies on graduating."

— Emma Douglas

Tapping into the talents of young people from different demographics

Each year, thousands of young people come into the investment and savings industry from University. However, a considerable majority of these graduates come from just a handful of institutions. Most are from families who either have contacts or a background in the sector; or who, because they are relatively well off, are well-versed in how the sector works.

So, what happens to the tens of thousands of talented young people who don't have this background or "leg up"? Currently, many are being lost to the sector at the first hurdle: they either never apply or get knocked back at the CV stage.

Shruti Khandekar and Emma Douglas

Early Careers Workstream Leaders

Trying to open up the pool of potential talent is the focus of the "Early Careers" workstream, led by Shruti Khandekar and Emma Douglas. And, as they make clear here, they have decided that a narrow focus can achieve the best results in the short term.

Our workstream has been going for four years now, and rather than try and cover all of the factors that can hinder young people from different backgrounds coming into the sector in one go – such as gender, ethnicity or neurodivergence – we're focusing on just one big cross-cutting issue in the first instance: social mobility.

Critically, we felt this was a hidden problem, one which companies probably aren't even aware of because the data to demonstrate that young people from disadvantaged backgrounds aren't making it through – especially to revenue-generating functions – isn't always captured.

Neither of us comes from a "disadvantaged" background in the classic sense of the word, but we did go to State schools and without any family background in the sector. Unaware of all the different opportunities in the industry, we both had to work that bit harder to find out about it and be successful "fitting in" when we did so – it must be even tougher for students who don't have the emotional support and push towards education that both our families could offer us.

The demographic we are targeting are first- and second-year university students from state school rather than private school backgrounds. In particular, those from lower socio-economic demographic backgrounds who wouldn't have been exposed to the investment and savings industry growing up because of their family backgrounds and education – and so probably would never even consider it as a career.

Our aim is to identify them early on in their University careers – ideally their first year – gain their interest and broaden their knowledge of the sector, provide mentoring and support with getting internships and interviews, giving them the tools they will need to be taken on by companies on graduating. Most importantly, we want to support them in building the confidence to apply for roles and do as well in interviews as their more resourced peers.

As with all the workstreams, we have to recognise what we can do on our own... and when we should be reaching out for specialist help.

We could see early on that we didn't have the contacts or the resources to identify suitable young people, so over 2019, we developed a programme in partnership with a social mobility charity called upReach, whose mission is "to help disadvantaged students from across the UK to realise their potential".

They already know the relevant societies on campus and careers officers, and how to access the relevant young people by asking the right questions. They can bring students from across the country into a common pool, filtered on their socio-economic status. They also provide the crucial pastoral support for the students, in addition to the support the students will receive from their mentor.

There are successful programmes – like Investment 2020 run by the Investment Association – which are already working very well across schools and in supporting the non-university routes into the investment sector. The same breadth of diversity in young hires has not yet found its way into the "traditional" internship and graduate roles, which require undergraduate degrees.

Furthermore, for the latter roles, when companies do move away from the usual Universities to try and attract a wider range of students, the tendency is to go to the other end of the spectrum and try and find students from very disadvantaged backgrounds, or provide support at an earlier stage in the education process to sixth formers in the most disadvantaged areas. That's not wrong for a moment, but the cultural challenge of bringing in somebody from an environment where they may even struggle to finish school is quite difficult. I think, change can be more successful if we go to the "missed middle" group of universities – which are very good ones, but maybe with students from a slightly different background and who bring a perspective not reflected in the industry today.

Is progress being made?

The programme is going very well. Students take part in a series of events across the first year, designed to give them a better understanding of the industry and the different roles available. Alongside that, each student gets a mentor from a firm who helps them with mock interviews, CVs and provides any general support required; whether with applications or even understanding workplace etiquette. We also hold an "Academy" – two days of events, exercises and speakers to build both students' technical investment knowledge and soft skills. The programme then concludes with an awards ceremony to celebrate the students' success over the year.

For the first year, we had over 25 firms involved in some way or another, supporting around 100 students from 36 different UK Universities, who have been filtered by up-Reach. Some have completed successful virtual internships; the rest are still in mentoring or early stages. Unfortunately, COVID-19 hampered an in-person work experience week for the students. However, several firms were able to provide a very successful virtual work experience week alternative in the summer of 2020. It is likely the work experience week in 2021 will also be virtual for the new cohort of students. Whilst it was a shame the students weren't able to get a flavour of what it's like to work in an office, something that many will have never experienced before, it was great to see how quickly the firms were able to turn the work experience virtual so the cohort did not miss out on this really important opportunity.

From the initial pilot scheme with 100 students, we have now increased this to 170 students in total across our first and second year of the programme. We are continuing to support the first cohort of students – they maintain a mentoring relationship and attend virtual sessions to keep up-to-date on key developments in the industry. We're also re-running the first year of the programme with new students, albeit all virtually. It's fantastic to have yet more firms (over 30), mentors (from 100 to 170) and volunteers involved in the programme, with enthusiasm and support for it growing as well.

We can't guarantee that these students will get jobs, but we're giving them work experience to put on their CVs, and so, at least they'll get through the door. You can't tell firms to take these students, but they do have a better chance of their potential being seen. Over time, that provides an opportunity to address the disproportionate situation we now see. We're confident that by equalising the opportunities on offer to all undergraduates in the UK, (rather than targeting an equalised outcome) we will find no shortage of talented, capable students whose perspectives and drive bring in the diversity that this industry needs in order to continue to be successful.

What can firms do to tap into this talent pool?

1. Be open-minded at the CV and interview stages. Look beyond the usual colleges and the practised polish and recognise that someone from a red brick university may have all the talent and energy – and has had to work harder to get there.

2. Try to think how you can get the best group of people, not just the "best people". You don't need to hire 20 graduates who all want to be the next CEO. You only need one or two of them. If you had to recruit a cohort of graduates or interns, what different skill sets do they need? Taking that approach would build in the diversity that would actually make your organisation better.

3. Try to break the (natural) inclination to appoint someone "like you". Look at someone with a different experience of life: that's what you need to avoid "groupthink" in your business.

4. Consider the benefits to clients. We all have very different clients now – they aren't just white, middle-aged men. We need people who can get the best outputs tailored to their needs, and who can better reflect the person opposite them...

5. Look at your job specs. Many companies make a maths or economics degree a default. But in lots of roles, you don't need beyond A-level maths. Rethink what the actual skill requirements are before you set the bar...

6. Look at the transferable skills that the candidate has, such as those acquired from part-time jobs and voluntary work they've done and consider which might be useful to your business.

Working families

A personal perspective

There are various ways to define a "working family"; but, for the purposes of this book, it's any single person or couple trying their best to combine work with caring responsibilities. That definition, of course, cuts across a great many other "groups", but there are some very specific challenges connected to trying to achieve a work/life balance when you have the pressure of holding down (let alone advancing) a career whilst also having a family member relying on you, or should you want to share parental care.

It's a situation that many of us will find ourselves grappling with in our working life and not just when we have children: while the Working Families has "parked" the challenge that many carers of elderly relatives face, that is a dilemma set to increase significantly over the years ahead as the population ages and formal support networks come under increasing pressure.

How our employer helps us deal with these situations can prove critical. It was certainly a challenge that has special relevance to my own career. In truth, it's arguable whether I would be CEO of the company I now run... or, indeed, have been inspired to write this book... had it not been so important to me personally.

In 2002, I was with Russell/Mellon in Lower Regent Street: the UK company I had been working for had recently been acquired, and this posed a problem. I had young children and wanted to play as full a part as I could in their early years. I had previously negotiated that I would work from home but come in once or twice a week on my own hours. However, the US business wanted me in the office every day because that was how they worked.

As a compromise, we agreed that I could come into the office each day at half-seven and leave at four: that would, at least, enable me to get home in time to bath the children and put them to bed. So, I had gone from (what was at the time) a very flexible UK employer to working for a very rigid US one; but I had at least been given some sort of compromise, even if it meant a daily two-hour commute.

But each day when I left at four, all I got from my colleagues was abuse about "working half days" – despite the fact that I'd put in an hour and a half ahead of them. And it was that experience which led me, at the age of 32, to give up my city salary and set up as a self-employed individual working from home. It meant a big drop in income, but I could walk my children to pre-school, pick them up and be with them for a few hours each evening... working furiously in between!

I managed to maintain that regime for five years before the business started to grow – and I got sucked back into working in an office again!

In order to be part of my children's lives at a time which is hugely bonding, my only option was to leave the company. Would that still be the case? You would think that in the 20 years since that, the industry would have moved on to accommodate male employees having to commute into and out of central London and wanting to see their young families, as well as make life easier for the many women holding down a career while shouldering a large part of the family care duties.

However, that's not what I heard when I was interviewing Claire and Sascha, as you'll see below. Yes, there are some companies that really are family-friendly, some that have family-friendly policies which get stuck at the management level, and some that have a long way to go in all regards.

Arguably when I faced that challenge, the most pressure came from my peers, but that was because it was the prevailing culture, and a company's culture stems from the top. They were still going out for beers after work and couldn't understand why I didn't want to come out on a Thursday and effectively chose the family over them.

But if the employer cared, they'd stamp on that sort of thing. I certainly would if I saw it going on today.

Claire Black and Sascha Calisan

Working Families workstream Leaders

What are the challenges that you've personally faced as working parents?

Claire: For me, the problems of combining work and raising a family started even before my first child arrived eight years ago: I had fertility treatment, and I didn't receive the support from my employer that I thought I would have. In fact, I was told that, because it was "elective surgery", I would get five additional days' leave and that was it – regardless of how many attempts I would need.

All of which made a highly stressful situation even more difficult, and stress is the last thing you need at that point in your life.

After that, I encountered the pressures that most women face. You return from maternity, and there's an expectation that you're just going to jump back into your job 100%. It doesn't work like that. As well as having to get back up to speed, part of your brain is taken up with babies. The pressure of trying to get everything done, then rushing off to pick up your child, is enormous.

In addition, of course, taking maternity leave impacts your career progression: there is this assumption that you are no longer so committed to your role and your career.

I came back to work four days a week because it was all I could possibly do: I was exhausted. However, that was made more complicated because, during my pregnancy, my marriage broke down and I became a single parent. I quickly had to go back to working five days because I couldn't financially support myself on a 20% pay cut.

So, coming back there was an extra pressure that I had to do this: it's my job keeping the roof over our heads.

My line manager was aware of my situation during my maternity leave, but I didn't have any one-to-one follow-up support to check on how it was working for me. I was still breastfeeding, so I was expressing at work and had to fit that around meetings. This was uncomfortable as well as difficult. I know companies do accommodate that and have a lactation room; but if you're made to feel guilty, or you don't have that window to go and do that when you need to, that makes it very, very difficult.

All this is going on while you want to keep performing for your company. I felt this pressure that I was still expected to do my job – and exactly how I did it when I left. And I am a high-performing individual, focussed on my career.

For me, it was really important to take my son to school one day a week so I would have that touchpoint with his teachers, so I had to apply for flexible working, and even then, it was reviewed every three months. At one point, it was taken away from me for a year because it was felt that, being a line manager myself, I had to be visible to my team, even though I had people in my office who had line managers in the US.

Having support internally at this critical time would have made a huge difference to me.

But there was no real conversation about my role changing in any way. All that said, this was eight years ago and certainly, in my case, the people and support have changed since then. I've had an extremely difficult time this year – and my line manager has been very supportive.

Sascha: I was in a similar situation in having multiple miscarriages over the course of seven years and became physically ill as a result of trying to work my way through it. There were times when I'd be in hospital, having had a miscarriage, on a work call making a presentation. It was bonkers. But I didn't want them to know that I was pregnant, or even thinking about becoming pregnant.

I got myself really ill with chronic fatigue. After a while, my GP signed me off. After two months, I went back to her. She asked me how I was, and I said, "A bit better, but now I'm pregnant..." "Right," she said. "You're absolutely going to have this one," and signed me off for another three months. I did have the baby, but the little monkey came out eight weeks early, so I had problems at the other end as well!

Because of the way women have been perceived in the workplace, you don't want to acknowledge that you're trying to have a family. And a lot of the reason why women are having fertility issues is because of the additional stresses involved.

What's the advice here? One is always anxious about mentioning pregnancy for the first three months to

anyone, let alone your employer, because of the elevated risk of miscarriage.

Sascha: There are a lot of conflicting issues here, but I think there just has to be more openness, that "this is us". Everybody's affected by it. The majority of people at some time in their lives are going to be building a family and it's just got to become part of the supported norm in the workplace.

Claire: And, obviously, if you are having fertility treatment, you need to let your employer know as you will need time out of work. However, another difficulty is because you're making yourself vulnerable, suddenly you can find yourself not being given the opportunities.

How easy was it for you to get your careers back on track?

Sascha: My experience at this point was different from Claire's. Our children are the same age, but I wasn't a single parent when I returned. I went back in a flexible way – one day working from home at first, then building up to two days at home, and I did from eight until four so I could fit in childcare.

I work at Northern Trust and they have one of the best family-friendly policies and are always trying to improve it. There was a lot of support for the practicalities.

When you are constrained in time, you are very focussed on getting your head down and doing the job at hand: you won't find many people coming back from maternity leave and not delivering. In fact, they become very efficient, and actually, a more effective member of the workforce in many ways. They can't do the list of 20 things they'd normally do, so they focus on the really important things.

But one thing that women often don't do as well as men in normal times is the networking. Men will naturally find ways to network while women are more reticent. And when you're time-constrained, that doesn't happen at all. I'm trying to mentor women to take out at least half an hour a week and reach out to somebody you're not working with... whether that's taking a coffee, or whatever. You owe it yourself to do that.

You forget about yourself because suddenly you are all about your child, and getting home and doing that family time. Your career is almost bottom of the list. You do your job because you need the income, and you do it well. Then, when you have more time because they are in school, and you're ready for your next step up, no one thinks about you because you're not on their radar. You've just been a "steady performer".

The importance of taking that time, having that coffee, thinking strategically, making sure people know what you're working on... all that goes to the bottom of women's lists. It's not just about the tools that they give you to come back to work — flexible working, emergency childcare — but also what you need to keep your career path going.

One of the things that Northern Trust did well was a maternity leave returner course, and it included creating your own brand. You forget that when you have a gun to your head. We're now talking about having a mentor even before you go off on maternity leave, to keep the lights on.

All that said, even now I'm back and doing well, I feel as though I lost five years.

So, should companies be doing more to facilitate networking - inside and outside the company?

Claire: It's a combination of encouraging networking to keep you current and connected, and mentoring to make sure you are doing all the right things. It doesn't have to be a huge investment in time, just making sure people are doing it.

What is the root of the problem?

Sascha: You might have the best HR policies on flexible working, but it does come down to the individual managers. And I know female managers who work flexibly themselves who won't let their teams work flexibly. It's not just men. It's females doing it to other females.

It can be a lack of perspective, and some of it must be around trust. Covid has now made people realise just how many jobs can be done flexibly. If it's a problem with your manager, then they too need some form of support as they have not always had the experience of people returning from maternity leave.

Coming back after a year can almost be like starting a new job again. It's just that you happen to know the people! It's a lot of information to take in, and when your brain capacity is not firing on all cylinders, it's really exhausting. Your manager needs to know what you're going through if they are to give you the support you need and to help you work in a way that would be most effective for you and them.

And they need to listen when you have that conversation.

Is "working families" a male challenge as well as a female one?

Sascha: When we set the scope for this workstream, we felt it was really important to bring in the working dads, as dads taking Paternity Leave bring- a whole load of different issues... not least the whole debate around whether or not it's the "done thing". Maybe Covid has pushed that forward. But there are not enough men doing it, and often the dad is the higher income-earner.

We have split the workstreams: one looking at the challenges that women face and the other at paternity leave and, specifically, shared parental leave. Where it can be made to work, it's fantastic in terms of shared careers, the dad being involved from the outset.

Will the lessons learned during Covid help you get to where you want quicker?

Sascha: It has accelerated flexible working, and positive management attitudes towards that are a big part of what working families need to combine both roles. To have men put on their out-of-office email that they are not available "as they are providing childcare" is just so fantastic. Execs now realise that you ARE productive working from home, not skiving or doing the laundry. It's done wonders on that side.

Claire: All the pressures that working families come under were really highlighted during lockdown. We didn't have to get into the office, but we still had to juggle work and looking after our children throughout the day, and keeping their education going too. It really showed just how dependent we are upon having structures in place to make achieving the balance possible.

Looking forward, what needs to happen for employers to support working families?

Sascha: We've demonstrated that things can be done differently – now, it's important that conversations are held, that mentoring is made available and ways are found to make it work for them as well as the employee.

Claire: It's important to remember that it's not a one-size-fits-all. Line managers need to be in touch with each of their staff's personal situations because otherwise, they can't begin to understand. The other side of it is that employees have to come forward too – like Sascha, I'm not always very good at saying what my situation is. If your line manager isn't in tune with the fact that there's something going on for you, or ask you the question, they'll assume that you're fine.

Sascha: Part of it is down to trust, as well as understanding. When I went back to work eight years ago, the manager assumed that I would be having a fairly easy time as I was working flexibly. Part of it is organisation. Part of it is peer support, and mentoring groups can be especially helpful for getting people through issues such as menopause… which is another thing people don't want to talk about!

And, really, it's about all areas of life. We need people to come together and openly talk about these things as challenges that most of us will face at some point and to help each other.

It's about treating each person as an individual with a life outside of work. It's about employers looking after that whole circle of life.

Chapter 5
Neurodiversity

"Without falling into stereotypes, there are some very distinct skills which come with neurodiversity. Those with dyslexia, for example, often have very good people skills and a creative, entrepreneurial mindset. Autism can often mean good problem-solving. Those with ADHD process information very quickly. Dyspraxia often goes with an ability to organise things and construct processes differently and being very creative because of that."

— Meike Bliebenicht

If "cognitive diversity" is a management aim within a business, then neurodiversity has to play a role: a relatively new aspect of overall workplace diversity, it takes on board the differences in the way our brains are "wired".

From an organisational point of view, these variations in cognitive functioning can increase diversity of thought and reduce groupthink, as well as provide ready access to often sought-after skills: these are people with a mindset that means they look at things in a different way, and who question established ways of thinking and working.

The neurological set-up of people with – for instance – autism spectrum disorder (ASD), ADHD and dyslexia results in many distinct and special qualities that accompany the very real challenges - ranging from creative thinking to process structuring.

When we understand and value this potential, we can access a world of opportunities.

The word "neurodiversity" was first used in the late 1990s by journalist, Harvey Blume, and autism advocate, Judy Singer. In 1998, Blume wrote in The Atlantic[5]: "Neurodiversity may be every bit as crucial for the human race as biodiversity is for life in general. Who can say what form of wiring will prove best at any given moment?"

In his book "Neurodiversity"[6], Dr Thomas Armstrong writes: "Instead of pretending that there is hidden away somewhere a perfectly 'normal' brain to which all other brains must be compared, we need to admit that there is no such brain... in fact, diversity among brains is just as wonderfully enriching as biodiversity and the diversity among cultures and races."

---

[5] September 1, 1998 issue of The Atlantic
[6] The Power of Neurodiversity: Unleashing the Advantages of Your Differently Wired Brain (published in hardcover as Neurodiversity) Cambridge, MA: DaCapo Lifelong/Perseus Books, 2011.

He goes on to talk about the need to create a discourse whereby labelled people may be seen in terms of their strengths as well as their weaknesses. "Dyslexics, for example, can be seen in terms of their visual thinking ability and entrepreneurial strengths. People with ADHD can be regarded as possessing a penchant for novel learning situations. Individuals along the autistic spectrum can be looked at in terms of their facility with systems such as computer programming or mathematical computation."

So how can our sector tap into this resource?

At the moment, most work environments and practices are distinctly geared against someone with a neurodivergent brain: our hiring processes, management techniques and workplace procedures have been created by and for neurotypical brains. Even if the person gets past the interview process, they are likely to find the "traditional" way of working antipathetic to the way they can best function.

Neither has it been a helpful assumption within society as a whole to equate neurodiversity with impaired mental health. They are not the same. That said, neurodivergent individuals may be more prone to certain disorders than the general population. For example, anxiety disorders have a high prevalence among individuals on the autism spectrum. In part, this can be attributed to the challenges and frustrations experienced when trying to navigate a neurotypical world.

Retaining the talents of neurodivergent people does require an understanding on the part of the employer to recognise potential problems and, where necessary, design them out of the individual's work environment.

The good news is that more firms are now recognising the importance of neurodiversity in the workplace by bringing a different way of thinking to teams.

Meike Bliebenicht

Neurodiversity Workstream Leader

If someone's brain works differently, they solve problems differently. They may spot things that other people do not see.

— Meike Bliebenicht

I have ADHD (attention deficit hyperactivity disorder) and, being the proud owner of a neurodivergent brain, I am thrilled by the benefits that neurodiversity will bring to our industry. By leading the Diversity Project's neurodiversity workstream, I aim to improve understanding of this potential to enable us to make better use of neurodiversity's important contribution to overall diversity of thought.

I'm currently Global Product Director at AllianceBernstein, having previously spent 10 years at HSBC Global Management. Before that, I was at J.P. Morgan Asset Management in Frankfurt and London for seven years.

The word "global" in my job title has meant a lot of travelling. It's also an arena where there is always short-term volatility. This type of job really suits me. I love everything which is super-dynamic... getting to the office and thinking this is my to-do list; then, after five minutes, everything is shuffled around. I thrive on short deadlines - anything which is highly energetic and dynamic.

But I find it hard to deal with things that aren't like that, really, to the extent where it freaks me out. Tasks which do not involve any activity on my side, such as having to read through piles of documents or listening to lectures, can actually make me quite anxious.

I always found that a bit odd. But while I have always had ADHD, I haven't always known it. What you are aware of from very early on is that - somehow - you're different. That can make you the outsider because you struggle with things that others take for granted. Equally, certain things come to you very easily. For instance, I used to wonder why everybody else around me would get nervous before making a presentation to a large audience. To me, that's the quietest moment of my life. Why does nobody else feel that way?

But then, other people can quietly sit in a corner for hours and read research papers or microanalysis — something I struggle with. Especially hard for me is getting things into my head that I'm not particularly interested in: my brain is always trying to find more interesting things to do. I used to try and cover it up, because you can't turn up at a business meeting and say, "Sorry, but that paper was unbelievably dull so I really couldn't get myself to read it..."

I don't like the word "condition" when people talk about ADHD, autism and so on, because in the diversity context, it's just a different way of being. It's not something wrong or something we need to cure, but you end up doing a lot of covering up because you don't want to stand out, especially not in a negative way. And because of that, rather like a duck swimming apparently effortlessly, beneath the surface there's an awful lot going on.

Doing all of that paddling just to appear "normal" can be exhausting.

You observe your peers and try to adopt their behaviours, all the time wondering why it's so hard for you. "Everyone in this meeting is relaxed except for me — and I'm anxious about getting found out." That's very common among people who have autism, ADHD, dyslexia and so on - especially those aged over 35 because they very likely didn't get a diagnosis as a kid.

A lot of people actually get diagnosed because of something else: all of this covering up and additional work can affect your mental health. They are struggling with anxiety or depression, go to their GP and are referred to a psychiatrist, then discover there is something else triggering this.

For our industry, this is one of the biggest challenges: you can't, for instance, see whether someone is dyslexic. ADHD is, at some point, visible... for instance, I use my hands a lot when I'm talking! But you would normally notice this and think it's just one of my special features and wouldn't associate it with different brain wiring.

High functioning autism is similar. There can be distinct physical movements associated with autism, and avoidance of eye contact, but they're not severe enough for someone to say, "There's something different about your brain". They will just assume that you don't like small talk, and sometimes this is held against you as if you just don't care... or you don't have any "team spirit".

There seems to be some sort of unwritten rule that every person in the same job at the same level of seniority must have developed a similar skill set over time, and act and behave in a certain way. If you don't, this is often pointed out to you. In most cases, such feedback is well-meant. But not accepting that there are many different ways of getting the right result is one of the main obstacles to successful neuroinclusion.

What progress is being made – and what more needs to be done?

Neurodiversity is now being talked about a lot more in the press and elsewhere because there is a very obvious benefit: avoidance of groupthink, having a different perspective, challenging conventional ways of doing things. If someone's brain works differently, they solve problems differently. They may spot things that other people do not see.

Without falling into stereotypes, there are some very distinct skills which come with neurodiversity. Those with dyslexia, for example, often have very good people skills and a creative, entrepreneurial mindset. Autism can mean good problem-solving. Those with ADHD process information very quickly. Dyspraxia often goes with an ability to organise things and construct processes differently and being very creative because of that.

In their 2018 report[7], the CIPD reported that Microsoft, JPMorgan, EY, Google, SAP, DXC Technology, Ford and Amazon were all running neurodiversity-at-work initiatives, and that these pioneer organisations have demonstrated early successes. "J.P. Morgan, for example, reports that 'after three to six months working in the Mortgage Banking Technology division, autistic workers were doing the work

---

[7] https://www.cipd.co.uk/Images/neurodiversity-at-work_2018_tcm18-37852.pdf

of people who took three years to ramp up — and were even 50 percent more productive'."

Neither does employing neurodivergent staff necessarily mean major investment. Back to the CIPD paper[8], where they report that: "Employers surveyed by the US Job Accommodation Network found that as many as 59% of common adjustment types cost nothing for the employer. Technology, in particular assistive tech in the form of iPad apps such as speech-to-text software, is facilitating both the inclusion and performance optimisation of neurodivergent people such as non-verbal autistic people."

Within the investment industry itself, we are moving away from expecting the exact same skills profile or how we should all behave. But so far, these have been baby steps. It's going to take time.

While having someone who is neurodivergent as part of a cognitively diverse team is an obvious asset, it is often questioned whether we necessarily make good people leaders.

I think this takes us back to the earlier point that there is often a certain expectation of how senior leaders should behave and the skill set they should have acquired. Of course, there are good leaders with neurodiverse brains.

---

[8]https://www.cipd.co.uk/Images/neurodiversity-at-work_2018_tcm18-37852.pdf

Most neurodiverse brains are very authentic and extremely loyal. For me, these are two very important attributes of good leadership.

Again, the bigger problem is whether you are able to progress beyond a certain level, because then there is still the expectation that you deal with a lot of information, for example; that you keep up to date with a lot of things going on around you; then just delegate the tasks and somehow follow up.

That's something that a lot of those with neurodivergent brains will struggle with because they often have problems with something called "executive functioning", which takes place in the pre-frontal cortex. So, tasks such as planning, organising, modelling outcomes – while not impossible – can take a lot of energy. In particular, tasks related to organising and planning do not have to be a struggle; some help with admin can already make a huge difference.

But again, we still live in a world where struggles with these perceived 'simple' tasks are often interpreted as weaknesses or showing reduced ability. And being judged, and sometimes written off like this might make it difficult for someone to really progress in higher levels of management.

This is a challenge which needs to be addressed urgently. From a business perspective, getting neurodivergent people in the right roles is critical. For instance, one of my first jobs was within a team called "Strategy and Planning", where, as far as I was concerned, nothing ever happened! I'm sure it had some sort of purpose, but I simply couldn't relate to it. They would get together in meetings and talk about things that might be happening in five or ten years' time, and how to prepare for that. I was thinking, "But we have more pressing problems – like what to do tomorrow."

I totally get that we need to do it and that other people want to do it. But it just wasn't me. I got to the point where I was exhausted. It was just draining to do this pointless exercise.

But then the financial crisis came along and suddenly, we moved into firefighting crisis management mode. I woke up from my one hundred years' sleep in Strategy & Planning and rolled my sleeves up. It was at that point that it clicked: this was the type of job I need... something highly energetic, dynamic, immediate. Where all people will go through the process of finding out what they enjoy / don't enjoy, for people with our type of brain, it's a bit more extreme.

I don't need a crisis every day, but I do look for something which has a certain level of energy all the time, and I don't find that exhausting at all. It's what I'm naturally good at, what I need to do to survive. That's why I looked for a job that could fulfil all of this – where I could travel, meet new people, make presentations, interact with the press, sometimes write an article… a lot of different things, and where no day is like another.

How can employers harness the potential of neurodivergence in the workplace?

In their 2018 report, the CIPD[9] defines what it describes as "The neurodiversity paradigm". In their words: "This is a perspective on neurodiversity that suggests neurodiversity is the result of natural human variation, and that there is no one 'normal' brain type. [It] stands in contrast to the highly medicalised perspective (until recently, the dominant perspective globally) that views autism, ADHD, and others as 'disorders' to be treated."

Is neurodivergency a "disability"? Not unless you expect me to act in exactly the same way as everyone else. Instead, it should be seen as a distinct skills profile, and you will need to provide assistance to overcome some of the challenges; but this will also enable you to access the massively positive skills and attributes that come with it.

The CIPD report goes on to estimate that 10% of the UK population has some form of neurodivergent brain[10]. That means that there are going to be a lot in our industry

---

[9] https://www.cipd.co.uk/Images/neurodiversity-at-work_2018_tcm18-37852.pdf
[10] https://www.cipd.co.uk/Images/neurodiversity-at-work_2018_tcm18-37852.pdf

already who will be neurodivergent. But as, for instance, only 16% of autistic adults in the UK are in full-time employment, according to the National Autistic Society, while a significant majority (77%) of unemployed autistic people say they want to work[11], there's obviously a long way to go.

The first challenge for a neurodivergent individual within the investment and savings industry is getting into the industry – and that means navigating the recruitment process. The tests will be standardised – and any standardised approach won't work for people who think differently.

If you get past psychometric testing, the technique of rapid-fire questions which change topic very quickly is more challenging than for those with neurotypical brains. People with autism may get so absorbed in a topic that they want to keep on talking about it.

That said, you can't change the recruitment process overnight. How do you improve it for neurodivergent candidates without potentially disadvantaging somebody else? This is probably a longer-term project where we will have to gain some more experience first. But a big step in the right direction would be to increasingly develop understanding and acceptance that not everyone is the same,

---

[11] www.autism.org.uk/get-involved/media-centre/news/2016-10-27-employment-gap.aspx

and hence, there cannot be a one-size-fits-all approach to recruitment.

But once you make it over the initial hurdle and you get into the job, onboarding and retention of neurodivergent brains are equally important. This will often be down to your line manager - how flexible they are, how good they are at managing a team to their strengths, and not expecting the exact same thing from every single person in the team. I had a fabulous manager at HSBC, who was really supportive, and I didn't need any formal adjustments because we would just figure it out between us, and he would let me focus on the things that I am best at.

There can also be an issue of people being reluctant to disclose that they are neurodivergent, not least because they may well have suffered badly during childhood for "being different". It can help just by talking about the topic, and the benefits provided by different thinking styles, more openly: most of us will either have a family member or know someone well who is neurodivergent. Senior leaders talking about that, making it normal, talking about the real positives, helping others understand it, and how it can make a team stronger... all that will encourage others to come out.

Making small accommodations in the workplace can also help retain staff because they will then be working under less stress. Bright office lights, for example, can contribute to sensory overload. Noisy open-plan environments can be highly distracting. Computer screens can be too bright. Hot desking can pose a problem for those who like to have their own dedicated work area.

But we are making progress, slowly but surely. And there is a big prize at stake: get it right, and businesses can really benefit.

Neurodiversity top 10 pointers

To attract neurodivergent candidates and to be able to fully benefit from the neurodiverse make-up of their workforce, investment management firms should consider the following.

Recruiting neurodivergent talent:

1   Simplify job descriptions: they should be concise, with clear distinctions between must-haves and nice-to-haves.

2   Demonstrate that neurodivergent talent is welcomed: include case studies on recruitment websites or state your commitment to neurodiversity in job descriptions.

3   Post job vacancies on dedicated websites: for example, the charity Autism Speaks[12] runs an online job board,

------

[12] https://www.autismspeaks.org/

and the LinkedIn group "The Spectrum Employment Community"[13] is dedicated to employment for people on the autism spectrum.

4   Review your interview technique: interviewers should be aware that neurodivergent candidates will often directly respond to the question asked and may not know how to expand in ways that will highlight their additional skills or experience. Training can help interviewers ask the right questions and interpret the responses they receive.

5   Provide direct feedback on interview performance: many neurodivergent candidates struggle to "read between the lines". It will help them if your feedback is concise and to the point. This applies in particular if you decide not to take forward discussions.

Retaining neurodivergent talent

6   Educate your team: neurodivergent colleagues often approach problems differently and come up with different solutions – sometimes quite radical ones. Without any knowledge of neurodiversity, there is a risk that such differences will be considered disruptive by other members of a team.

---

[13] https://www.linkedin.com/groups/5086843/

7   Tackle biases in the system: ensure that neurodivergent individuals are not disadvantaged because they do not seem "a good fit". Biases need to be tackled, not just in recruitment processes, but also with career progression and performance measurement.

8   Allow for some accommodations: simple changes can make a big difference, for example not having to hot-desk, or being able to work from home one or two days a week.

Developing neurodivergent talent

9   Provide career support: neurodivergent employees are often not aware of career opportunities, as they may struggle to understand an organisation's structure, or do not know how to network or what to say. Mentoring or coaching can help.

10 Provide leadership sponsorship: leadership drives inclusion, so hiring, retention and promotion efforts will be more successful if senior management teams are aware of the benefits of neurodiversity and are on board with your efforts to create a more inclusive workplace.

Chapter 6
LGBT+

"I looked around me and saw people who weren't just LGBT but also from different ethnic backgrounds. And I thought, this is the generation coming through. By connecting them together there was a massive opportunity for the industry to effect change... not just in the LGBT world but in ethnicity and gender as well."

— **Colette Comerford**

The LGBT+ workstream is comprised of an umbrella group made up of LGBT Great[14], InterInvest[15] and The Investment Association[16]. It has two collective goals:

- To develop LGBT+ diversity and inclusion across the industry.

- To identify and promote best practices to support LGBT+ people and allies.

[14] https://www.lgbtgreat.com/
[15] https://interinvest.org/
[16] https://www.theia.org/

While everyone reading this will know of The Investment Association, here's what you need to know about the other two groups;

LGBT Great is a specialist membership organisation focused on measuring and improving LGBT+ diversity and inclusion maturity within the investment and savings industry through insights, visibility and outreach programs. The initiative was launched in 2017 and has attracted global attention in three continents and grown into a community of 2,000 people across the industry.

Its aims are to:

- Make LGBT+ diversity and inclusion relevant to everybody
- Engage industry leadership on the LGBT+ diversity and inclusion agenda
- Develop innovative research, data and thought leadership insights
- Establish and amplify the visibility of LGBT+ and ally talent and member initiatives
- Substantiate improvement with fit-for-purpose industry metrics

InterInvest was established in 2018 to drive LGBT+ equality and inclusion across the investment industry in the UK and support similar initiatives globally.

It's aims are to:

- Provide an open forum for investment peers to discuss LGBT+ issues
- Share best practice within the industry and enable firm to firm mentoring to provide support to in-house LGBT+ networks
- Promote and influence LGBT+ inclusion across the investment industry
- Attract and retain LGBT+ talent into the investment industry
- Engage allies and promote allyship, drawing on other intersectional networks with similar experiences

You can find out more about both organisations on the Diversity Project website.

LGBT+: a personal perspective

For the first four years of my career, I worked closely with a colleague who became a friend. When he left to join another organisation, we met up for a beer, where he said, "I need to tell you something. I always wanted to – but was too scared to say. I'm gay."

I was really shocked. Not that he was gay, but that I'd always thought we had a really close relationship, and that he had never felt able to share that really important piece of information with me. Why not?

That was three decades ago, but in more recent times, another manager that I'd worked with for 10 years told me he was getting married to his male partner - and that was the first conversation that we'd had about him being gay.

I've always tried to have an open relationship with anyone and everyone I've worked with. But in both those scenarios, people that I thought I'd been quite close to had chosen not to share something quite significant with me. So, I'm thinking, what was my behaviour that stopped that conversation from progressing sooner?

My conclusion was that my colleagues were on their own personal journey and I had no idea of the challenges they may have faced in the workplace.

Colette Comerford and Matt Cameron

LGBT+ Workstream Leaders

Matt: For over 11 years now, I've worked within talent management across the investment, wealth management and savings industry. Prior to this, I read Medieval and Modern History at Birmingham. And before that, I lived in a small town called Lytham St Anne's, near Blackpool in Lancashire. I come from a working-class background and was the first to go to University from my family – so the first to break away from my roots.

As a gay man, I was also very much part of a minority group where I was brought up: until I went to University, I didn't know any other LGBT people. After Uni, I moved to London, not knowing what I wanted to do, and found it very difficult to access any of the big firms. I didn't have any contacts, and whilst I had a 2.1 from a red brick university, I didn't have one from Oxbridge.

I ended up in investment recruiting, and in the five years that I was there, we expanded from 8 to 120 people. I left in 2015 to set up my own diversity and inclusion recruitment business, The Ocean Partnership, joining forces with my co-MD, Clare Scott, who had a similar background to me. As well as recruitment and consultancy research, we moved increasingly into diversity and inclusion advisory – and that's why I started getting involved with the Diversity Project in 2016.

We ran some research looking at the barriers in terms of the LGBT+ agenda within the industry, and that's when we decided to develop a role-modelling programme called Project 1000[17].

We gained so much momentum that firms asked us to talk to them about the agenda, and we started to think about developing Project 1000 into a strategic offering. That became "LGBT Great" which we launched in January 2019

[17] https://www.lgbtgreat.com/role-models

with five founding members. Membership helped us to fund programmes and, as of today, we have 30 members - globally, as well as in the UK.

Colette: I'm Irish – I was born and grew up in a very small village, so, very similar to Matt in lots of ways. Even from the age of 3 or 4, I just felt different. I had a lot of challenging conversations with my mum around what I wore and what I did: this is how I learned to negotiate at a very early age! She wanted me to do Irish dancing, I wanted to play football... and just do what I was comfortable with. At that age, I was completely unaware of my feelings or how to express myself.

The turning point was around the age of seven. I explicitly said in my letter to Santa that I did not want a doll. But I got one anyway and called it Boy George. I thought: if he can wear nail varnish and lipstick, why does my mum have a problem with me wearing jeans and a t-shirt and playing football?

The whole family laughed, and I sort of shut down at that point. Back then, nobody understood what I was thinking or feeling; I never said any of this. But my grandma said to me: "Don't worry, Colette. You can call your doll whatever you want." I went away from that point thinking just always be yourself; stand up for what you believe in. My grandmother's always going to be there to support me.

I still have these challenges, but life just goes on.

Fast forward to when I was 17: I was really struggling at that point – feeling different, not having anyone around me to talk to. The expectation was that you got married and had 2.4 kids. I didn't see that. I played a lot of sports. Football was my safe place and I used that a lot in terms of my mental health.

As much as I loved my family, I knew I had to get away from this small town or close right down: escapism is quite a common theme in the LGBT+ community. Luckily, one of the people I played football with was a teacher and she said that Bank of Ireland ran apprentice-type training. So off I headed to Dublin: the big city.

I left Dublin when I realised that it too was a very small place and I still had no one to talk to about what I was feeling and who shared my experiences. I then moved to London and worked for Barclays, where I had an incredibly immersive experience working with international clients. But all the time I was there, my work and weekend lives never crossed over. LGBT+ and my partner were never spoken about.

In 2010, I ended up in Asset Management at M&G. The first week I was there, my manager took me for lunch with the rest of the team and asked me about myself, and if I had a partner. In that split second when you're asked a question like that, you use your risk-assessing ability, and I thought: "No one has ever asked me if I had a 'partner'... not 'boyfriend' or 'husband', but 'partner'".

So, I felt that I could actually say this now.

After that, small talk in the office was, "How was your weekend with your partner", and that was a massive turning point for me. It had taken a lot for me to say it, but I felt I could... because of that one question.

Moving on to 2014: The year before, I had my first experience of a contractor in my team experiencing homophobia, and she reported it to me. It was a really awful situation. It just didn't make any sense, but I had the support of my manager to help me through that. During conversations that followed about my personal development, my manager told me that if you're going to lead your team, it's going to be about trust. How many of them know about you? You let people in when you want to go bold. It's the starting point for innovation, change and transformation.

My manager knew from feedback that some people in M&G wanted to start an LGBT network and suggested I run it. I had no experience of creating a network, but thought that if I didn't do it, who would?

That first day, I went down the corridor to meet the others interested in being in a network and almost turned around through anxiety about who was going to be in the room. But guess what? They were all people I knew… and we just found each other. When you meet someone like you in the industry, it's like you've found a friend – because you both know where you're coming from.

In October 2014, we launched the LGBT network within M&G, and the next year they asked me to take on a broader D&I role: I didn't know anything about the other strands but thought: "I'm just going to have to be curious and learn".

In 2016, I joined the Diversity Project. One of the first conversations was with Matt, who had been a great supplier to us at Ocean, helping us to think about inclusion and diversity. After a few months, I thought that Matt might be gay, but I didn't really know.

Matt: Isn't it obvious?

Colette: So, I'm sat round the table at the Diversity Project and wondered: if I mention my partner's name, would Helena or anyone around the table ever talk to me again? Because you always have that fear – will this affect my career and my relationships with people? You just carry that with you. But Matt spoke up to say he'd be happy to lead on LGBT – and it took off from there.

We set up an LGBT meeting and had lots of people wanting to come – but were snowed off. By the time we actually held the first meeting, we had found even more people wanting to be part of it. I walked out from the talks into the lounge and one woman said to me, "I'm a black, gay woman working in the industry – what is there for me?"

Each of these on their own we are trying to address in our industry, so...

I looked around me and saw people who weren't just LGBT but also from different ethnic backgrounds. And I thought this is the generation coming through. By connecting them together there was a massive opportunity for the industry to effect change - not just in the LGBT+ world but in ethnicity and gender as well. That was the build-up to LGBT Great's launch – and since then, it has been incredible.

Matt: Like a domino effect.

Does either of you still experience homophobia within the industry?

Matt: Not necessarily direct attacks or homophobia. What we do experience is "micro-aggressions", where people say, "I know someone gay like you", or "I've got a gay cousin", or "That's so gay". It's basically a lack of understanding around the impact of language but does demonstrate positive intent. It is a case of not knowing 'how to' have the conversation.

Colette: Some use phrases like that because it was OK at school and they haven't moved on or realised it's not OK to say it now.

Matt: We've got over 500 role models now, and in total, I've probably heard only 20 or 30 horrendous experiences from industry employees, some, where employees have just had to leave. But these are few and far between and I don't think it's a particular reflection of our industry because I know this happens in other sectors too.

Colette: Our role is to send out a strong signal, to help the environment change and bring it into the modern world; otherwise, we won't attract and retain people.

The generation coming through are from environments where their friends are gay, there's sex education in school on LGBT+ and gender fluidity. And they are looking for employers – regardless of their own identity where this isn't an issue – because they are looking for equality in all its forms and what it stands for.

Young people are speaking up and standing up for each other.

Lots of staff are learning through their children. So, there's a massive opportunity to connect with that. They're also conscious through the stories we share – about how we've been affected and felt vulnerable. They don't want their own child to be struggling like that. They want an open conversation about what's going on in their mind and want to know how they can help them.

How much progress are you making?

Matt: What I see in the industry is that, while support for LGBT+ is not necessarily open or visible, when you actually ask the question, the people that you least think will be supportive actually are. Even in places like Republican parts of the States, execs will tell you that, while they've been brought up not to embrace LGBT+ equality, they know they have a duty or obligation to accept and to help everybody regardless, and they tell you what they've been doing to help LGBT+ colleagues. It's about acceptance of differences regardless of whether we agree.

Stereotype dictates that we are as vibrant as other industries, such as retail, travel, or music for example, but that's probably because of the profile of those coming into our sector: predominantly privately educated. I wouldn't say the industry isn't open or welcoming; it just needs encouraging and it needs showing how.

Colette: Now, gay and lesbian couples in their 30s have got married, had kids, so there's a change in the narrative from how things were when we started. They're breaking barriers in so many ways – and they're role models for the generation coming through.

We're not just talking about gay men or women, but bisexuality too. And you're finding out the backgrounds and different challenges that each of them has – in places like New York, Hong Kong, Singapore, and India. To step forward now is incredible: it feels like it has just ignited this whole piece and shone a light on the people who already existed... but nobody knew that important part of them.

What should middle managers be thinking about in terms of managing their teams? How should they be modifying their behaviour? And what behaviours should they be encouraging within their team?

Colette: Often, managers have been appointed because of their technical expertise rather than their proven management skills. The role of "manager" has moved on from just managing performance and deliverables. You have to move away from focusing on the technical... and focus on your people.

Managers need to connect with their people and understand their personal values... what drives them in terms of behaviours, and how that aligns with company culture. Even that one signal to me from my manager using neutral language enabled me to open up. Get to know your people and their strengths. You'll get a lot more out of people if you explore their minds and get to the bottom of the things they do outside of work.

What's more, clients are asking us more and more about the diversity of our teams. How do you make decisions? How do you avoid group think or apply better judgement? How do you show "difference"? What are you doing to increase workforce diversity? The pressure is now on managers who have to turn this corner, because otherwise, it will affect how you win, do, and retain business. Yes, it's all data-driven, but you have to get to the people behind that. It's a different world.

Matt: It all has to come down to inclusive management, leadership style and a team culture of equality. A team which is multi-generational, inter-sectional... and making it easy: breaking things down into actions that help team members experience empathy for others and including everyone in key decision-making. The middle manager has to lead by being the role model within the team who sets the right values and tone.

Vicarious reinforcement means that others will naturally follow and copy the leader if they are praised. We talk about allyship a lot as well. Not just in the context in the LGBT+. It's important that it's broader than that.

We constantly talk about The Five Traits of Impactful Allyship: Self-Discovery, Empathy, Courage, Responsibility and Persistence:

- The first one is around Self-Discovery, so you make sure you know what issues affect different groups;

- The second is around Empathy, how do we out ourselves in the shows of others and work to make everyone feel accepted and valued, regardless of identity?

- The next is around being Courageous and being prepared to make mistakes – and when your team sees you making a mistake, they feel it's OK to make mistakes too, but we just need to know how to apologise.

- We talk about Responsibility and Persistence as well... it can start off with loads of enthusiasm and passion, but everyone then gets busy. Rather than trying to crack all the nuts at once, work out what you can do each month and pursue that.

- Finally, it's important that we have commitment and engagement, and that this is owned by the manager, and therefore, we need a way to go back to those commitments, so they are accountable and checked in on regularly

Colette: Empathy, kindness, listening. Managers can look at the whole team, but you have to break it down and have a relationship with an individual. We never know what might have gone on in that person's life to make them feel vulnerable. I've had LGBT friends who haven't told me. But something may have happened to make them feel vulnerable and we need to break that down.

So, it's a bit of a minefield, but you have to start with the individual and build some trust. Share your own experiences, show some of your own vulnerabilities and hopefully, that will open things up.

Matt: People will sometimes not have the conversation for fear of not knowing what language to use and getting it wrong. It's absolutely OK not to know the ins and outs of language. And it's fine to get it wrong. Again, it's got to be role-modelled from leadership: to create a space where you can have those conversations… and sometimes get it wrong. And know how to apologise.

Generally, if you give that opportunity, people will embrace it!

Colette: One of the challenges is that LGBT+ has followed the same route as BAME (Black, Asian, and other minority ethnic groups), with everything chucked into one acronym. But by wrapping it all into one bubble, don't break it down, and we have our own unique differences – and challenges! For instance, there's a lot of biphobia – even within the LGBT community. And trans, non-binary identities are so far behind. So, we as a community have to do a lot more on language ourselves.

What would progress look like in a couple of years from now?

Matt: Our target is 1,000 individual role models – and we're halfway there now. We aim to show how they are helping to inspire and motivate others through their stories. We're one of the most energised workstreams and role-modelling is part of that. I must say a big thank you to Colette's leadership as LGBT Great's Lead Role Model Ambassador who has been instrumental in driving support across our industry.

Colette: You can't achieve anything unless everyone shares accountability. So, for me, progress would be everybody getting involved in some way from a D&I perspective.

One of the challenges with being a role model and being visible is that you are constantly coming out all the time. And a huge amount of energy goes into it. That's why we need this solidarity so that everyone comes together, and no one feels like they're carrying the flag alone.

Young people will come through as the narrative is changing and say - the problem is not us, it's you. So, we, as organisations, have to fix ourselves right now. If we want people with all of these values and strengths, then why would we blind-CV them, assess them the same way or take away their identity to fit in with us?

Chapter 7
Disability

"The purpose of the Disability Workstream is to accelerate progress towards an inclusive culture within the industry around disability: an inclusive culture that supports and celebrates disabled employees will lead to happier and more productive employees, who will thrive within a proactively inclusive environment. It will lead to effective teamwork, wider perspectives and better investment decisions."

— Diversity Project Goals and Priorities

Some 16% of working-age adults in the UK live with a limiting long-term illness, impairment or disability [18]. And while the most commonly-reported impairments are those that affect mobility, lifting or carrying,[19] there are many whose conditions are not immediately obvious.

The disability employment gap has reduced in recent years, but it remains massive: just over half of disabled people (53.2%) were in employment in 2019 compared

---

[18] Family Resources Survey 2010/11
[19] Family Resources Survey 2011/12

with just over four out of five non-disabled people (81.8%)[20].

How can this gap be bridged and attract and retain their talents within the investment and savings sector? We talk to three people who have helped take forward the Disability Workstream at the Diversity Project.

Katy Halliday

Disability Workstream Leader

While I don't personally have a disability, I was offered the chance to help lead the Disability Workstream because of my experience running employee networks, and I jumped at the chance.

I started work in the finance sector 22 years ago. I don't have a degree: I went to the careers office when I was 18, at my all-girls grammar school in South East London, not knowing what I wanted to do, and ended up working for Lloyds Bank in the Settlements Team. I held a variety of Operations roles in investment banking, before moving to asset management. About seven years ago, I joined L&G as an implementation manager, bringing new clients into the firm, then across to Blackrock to do the same role.

---

[20] Labour Force Survey, LFS 2019

At BlackRock, there's a really rich culture of employee-led networks right across the firm - from LGBT and Black through to Women's and Veterans networks; we've even got a Green Team. In 2016, Disability and Mental Health networks didn't exist within BlackRock. There was senior interest in forming a Network like this for employers, and I was asked by my line manager if I would bring my project management skills into the mix to help set up the new net-work.

I work for a great company, one with a fantastic platform to get new ideas across, and this gave me a chance to get even more involved in that side of things.

I met all the founders of the Network, including a lady in the US who identified as having a disability and has had a fantastic career: an MD and a real inspiration. She made me realise how awesome it would be to drive this issue forwards: people with disabilities have found themselves, for a long time, almost second-class citizens right across the world – not just in financial services. This was some-thing I hadn't really understood, but she brought it right to the surface for me and taught me why we should take the opportunity to make a stand and make a change.

I was heavily involved in the network for about 18 months, serving as a global co-chair, and then BlackRock asked me to represent them at the Diversity Project. When the lady running the disability workstream had to step down, I was asked to step in.

I did that for 18 months, and now, the DP has a partnership with Scope[21] to help drive it forwards. We decided to look at the whole of the employment lifecycle of a person with a disability: from talent attraction through to the interview process, the onboarding process, first day in the office, and then development and talent retention. And we should break it down to understand the barriers at each stage, as well as adding in people's personal stories and experiences as that lends real power to the message.

For that, we decided that we needed experts to come in, to understand our business and our challenges, and present something back in bite-sized chunks... almost a best-practice guide that Project members could reference and use.

Scope were keen to partner with us because they had found it difficult to get into the financial services sector: to be able to get through to so many companies in one go was really appealing to them, as well as opening up an opportunity to do a deeper dive with organisations that felt they needed more expert support.

---

[21] https://www.scope.org.uk/

The bottom line was that we wanted to showcase the best practice guidelines from the experts and ensure that all of our HR Managers and our line managers really do understand some of the challenges that people with disabilities face. We also wanted to help them feel comfortable to get into conversations with people and ask what they were doing wrong, what they were doing right, what could they do better, and how they could help that individual.

I think we did a pretty good job at nailing that. But just as we were about to hold an event to launch the toolkit, share what we'd learned and kick off the partnership, Covid hit. We did it online, where you will now find the toolkit, but it was obviously a bit of an anti-climax!

How ahead/behind is the sector compared with other professions in dealing with this?

I don't think we're behind, particularly: the sector is on a journey, like other employers in the UK. It's where LGBT was 10 years ago, and Gender 20 years ago. We're all trying to come up the curve together. I like to think that, because this is a well-trodden path, actually people are embracing it – they want to learn and educate themselves, rather than being frightened about it. It's a bumpy road to get there but we've done it with other workstreams. I am hugely positive about this.

One of the challenges is that not all disabilities are immediately visible, so that can make it harder to get a message across. This is why we need to promote education with our line managers, HR managers and our colleagues as well... that what you see is not necessarily what you get.

The drive for this needs to come from both within a company and from staff themselves. There are a number of reasons why employee networks are a good thing: as well as delivering change within an organisation, there are huge personal development opportunities. People telling their stories can also really help give it that extra punch.

It's also important for firms to recognise the total effect within the company and on people's perception of the business, talent recruitment and retention. I've just worked with our summer interns for 2020, and they really embrace the work of our employee networks – and almost expect it of a big company like BlackRock.

More and more, young people are holding us to account, not just for delivering a good product to our clients and being environmentally responsible when it comes to investing, but also being a good employer and enriching the communities in which we work.

Tim Roberts

Disability Workstream Leader

I was born profoundly deaf, and work in a mostly mainstream environment. Generally speaking, my progress has been hindered by a lack of assistive technology and people's attitudes towards disability. There is a stigma around this that is ingrained into people's mind from parents, grandparents etc. A good example is "You're deaf and dumb", which is an old saying and possibly not meant to be as offensive as it is today, but this was the saying back then and it is up to people like me to prove that this is not the case.

I work at HSBC, in the Global Marketing team, so I have a lot of meetings with people from different countries, and that can be quite challenging. Although, I find that many overseas people who can speak English tend to understand me better than those in the UK, and they are easier for me to understand too because they speak properly and don't abbreviate and use slang.

At times in my career, getting the right equipment – even a suitable tablet so that I can watch subtitles on one screen and do a presentation on another – has been a challenge, and has affected my performance. HSBC have been great at providing a range of stuff for me and I am thankful to work for such a great employer.

My other challenge has been awareness. If you have a disability, you have to do a lot more than just your job. When I have meetings, I have to book support (i.e., a Captioner to type up what is being said on the call). If I have video meetings, I need more time between calls to prepare but not everyone understands that. For those in a wheelchair, going to a meeting means planning your route, arranging support, taking more time to get there. Again, not everyone makes allowances and jams meetings together just because it suits them. At HSBC, we are working towards booking meetings for 50 minutes because even though we are not in a big building, people do still need that time to go to the toilet, etc. That is a basic need, and disabled people may need a bit more time.

Other people will have issues around light or noise levels in an office that can make it difficult for them to perform. Many will simply not be able to get to an office during rush hour, need to take time out for medical appointments or find it problematic to work a full working week, just as a working parent might want slightly different hours around their children's school hours, etc. This is why flexible working is so important.

If you want the talents of a particular person on your payroll, you need to find ways to make it possible.

The recruitment process has changed quite a bit, but a lot of companies still have a long way to go on accommodating different types of disability. For instance, I'd obviously prefer a face-to-face meeting where I can lip-read rather than a telephone one; someone in a wheelchair may prefer a video or telephone call. Companies need to look at the forms people fill in when they say they have a disability and liaise with them on how best to conduct any interview. I've arrived at a company and they clearly haven't even registered the fact that I'm deaf, despite filling this in on the application form.

Oddly, smaller companies have been better at responding to issues like this because there is less red tape to cut through, while bigger companies aren't always good at sharing experiences and best practices between departments, or even countries. At HSBC, in Global Asset Management, we have a Diversity and Inclusion Steerco to help identify areas of improvement and for people to share where things are working. No company is perfect, but I truly appreciate everything that HSBC are doing for me.

It's not all negative. People's attitudes now are different from when I started my career. Twenty years ago, people didn't care. Now, people are too politically correct and not sure what to do, so sometimes they take the easy way out – 'do nothing'. The best managers I have worked for are the ones who tackle this head-on and go "Right, this might be a challenge, but I like this person, I think they can do a good job for me and I will do everything I can to help them".

In the big wide world out there, there's a long way to go, but the fact that the Diversity Project is being taken seriously shows that the will is there.

Subira Jones

Diversity Project Disability Ambassador

Being a woman of Jamaican descent with a degree in Economics, I appreciate the great strides taken to expand diversity in the investment and savings industry, allowing me to pursue the career of my choice - irrespective of race and gender.

However, my medical condition has meant that I have met other barriers and led directly to me leaving my role as a Client Reporting Analyst and pursuing a career as a Burnout Prevention Consultant and Lifestyle Strategist, with the vision to help other talented professionals avoid burnout and debilitating work stress illnesses.

My experiences demonstrate just how difficult it is for anyone with a disability or chronic health condition to fulfil their potential within the sector without one critical factor being available to them: flexibility.

And, with some 20% of the population having some form of disability, 96% of which are "invisible", just how many talented people are currently not coming into the sector simply because of employers' inflexibility (real or perceived) around part-time and home working? How many are not moving on to more challenging roles because they can't negotiate the same flexible terms they have negotiated in their current job?

That's why I was delighted to become a Diversity Project Ambassador, and this is my story.

I call myself "The Corporate Hippie ™" because that's the juxtaposition between my analytical side (I enjoy working the investment world) but also being people-centred in how I do things. I've always felt I was a round peg in a square hole... but on the right board.

I took my degree at Swansea, but in my final year, my mother suffered a heart attack and went into a coma. I finished my degree then came back to London to spend some critical time with her. I wasn't in a position to take on a full-time, demanding job so I opted to waitress which allowed me to earn a living and have the flexibility to visit my mum in hospital.

My mother remained severely neurologically disabled, so in 2017, two years later, I decided it was time to get a "real job" - at Willis Towers Watson... but my mother passed away just as I was meant to start. I began work four days after her funeral.

In 2018, I began to have symptoms of MS – although I didn't know it was MS at the time. I lost the sight in my right eye, and my ability to walk, but I was able to carry on working for quite some time as WTW has a very flexible approach, so I could work from home and also attend hospital appointments.

My next job was with Jupiter Asset Management and it was there, while I was in my probationary period, that I was diagnosed with MS. They couldn't (then) offer the same level of flexibility, so it was a straight choice between my work and my health. I left and did manage to get the MS back into remission.

I found that I could work three days a week, but not full-time – at least, not without quickly reaching burnout. I started looking for another job but knew it was like finding the proverbial needle in the haystack. But I then realised: this SHOULDN'T be a needle in the haystack. There need to be more opportunities available to other people like myself who want to continue to work or get back in the industry… but almost every role is being advertised as full-time.

Disability is often looked at from the perspective of the people already in the workplace living with a disability…

not from that of someone wanting to get into the industry or even moving from one post to another.

It's also looked at purely in terms of capability rather than capacity. My problem – and that of many others – is capacity rather than capability. We can do an excellent job – just not five days a week.

With maternity leave and women returning, part-time working isn't totally alien to the industry and can be made to work in any job. So, let's go one step further, and make more jobs available part-time. It won't just help people like myself: we've got some amazing candidates who currently aren't in the market because they aren't able to work full-time for a variety of reasons.

So now my career is trying to help people who, like myself, are going through some sort of stress-related problem.

I don't think it was a coincidence that my MS came on after a period of huge personal stress: over 50% of days off in the UK are caused by stress-related illnesses. And one of the factors I try and get employers to consider is the whole person. You have life stresses, such as your personal finances, as well as work stresses. And your ability to manage both effectively enables you to perform in your job and achieve your aspirations while maintaining a healthy life.

When there's a lack of balance – which is what I had – is when you get burnout. It's the inability to make the distinction between coping with stress and managing stress. One is a short-term strategy, the other is a long-term solution and effective at avoiding burnout.

Wellbeing is a holistic thing, and I look at it as seven dimensions: physical, mental, emotional, spiritual, financial, social and occupational. Any approach has to integrate all these factors.

When I was first diagnosed with MS, I was very guarded when I spoke to HR – I didn't know how much I could and couldn't say. Their first loyalty is to the organisation. I needed to speak to someone who understood the world that I was in, but also liaise between myself and the organisation. That would have made a huge difference. A lot of people don't actually speak up about what they are experiencing which may be affecting their performance.

And again, it's not about capability but capacity. Talking to… listening to… your employees is the first step to making the most of, and retaining, your single biggest asset: the people who work for you.

Top pointers on how to recruit and retain the talent of people with disabilities

1. If someone with a disability applies for a post, make sure you take note of their disability and liaise with

them to work out in advance what they need to get to the interview… and have a level playing field with the other candidates in that interview.

2. Give them more time to get to meetings or prepare for them.

3. If they need additional resources, such as interpreters or lipreaders, or assistance getting to meetings, make those available.

4. Make sure the technology is in place to give them the best possible opportunity to perform well.

5. Recognise that many disabled people would really benefit from flexible working – either more home working or being part-time.

6. Talk to your staff on a regular basis to identify and iron out any problems that are arising. It might seem like a tricky subject to broach, and some managers are, understandably, anxious about "saying the wrong thing". But it's far better to be transparent and open.

Remember that there is no "one-size-fits-all" approach to enabling people with disabilities to work for you – each person will have different issues.

Mental Health

Katy Halliday describes the work now being done to promote good mental health within the investment and savings sector – particularly in the wake of Covid-19.

Mental Health is huge and, as a group, we say that your mental health should be treated as thoroughly as your physical health: it applies to everyone, and we all have to look after it.

It's such a wide remit that we are concentrating our efforts in one direction: not focussing on specific mental health conditions, or on people who have challenges with their mental health, but promoting awareness of what mental health is... and why it's important to individuals and to our respective organisations, as well as the benefits to employers in looking after the mental health of their employees.

Right at the start of lockdown, we ran some "ask me anything" sessions, talking generally about mental health and lockdown, and we soon realised that people were interested in a number of compartmentalised issues.

The first one is stress management – particularly finding ourselves in the new world of working from home and not having interactions in the office. A GP who specialises in stress management talked to the group about how they can be more mindful of their teams when they're under stress and how to manage stress in the workplace, particularly at a time when we didn't fully appreciate what was going on.

We're also looking at what to do as managers during lockdown and post-lockdown – particularly around the reintroduction of people back into the working environment. How do people feel about it, and how do they handle any conflicts of feelings they may have?

Something I'm taking personal responsibility for is domestic abuse during lockdown: we've agreed to put a spotlight on it because, all around the world, we've seen an exponential increase in domestic abuse, and we have heard concerns from various organisations that they do not understand it fully and do not have the resources available for their staff. We are hoping to work with a women's refuge organisation to get education and promotion out to the wider group, but also adding some storytelling and letting people know about the fantastic resources we have available. But that is very much work in progress.

We're also looking at the connection between mental health and ethnicity, working together with Gavin Lewis and with all of our respective organisations on how to speak about it, how to articulate it to staff and promote positive conversations.

Covid has highlighted mental health issues in the workplace that were there before: it's brought things to the surface and now we need to formalise and address these things. It's shown, for instance, the importance of the role of mental health first-aider, and we've seen a lot of interest in training and installing these across the industry.

There is always the concern that many people will have a natural disinclination to talk to someone within their own company because of the continuing perceived "stigma" of mental health problems, but I'd like to think that the world has moved on. Whatever you're trying to champion and change, you will always have pockets of resistance. But generally, there is more openness about mental health and disability in the workplace. People are still struggling a bit to know the right words to use. But they are more willing to listen and learn and to start to embrace breaking down the taboos.

Now, new folk coming through the door are a lot more open to it: our graduate interns ran a survey for me on their university experience regarding mental health provision, and they were all very open and honest, and happy to talk about it. That's infectious – and older members of staff are starting to listen to the youngsters.

At BlackRock, we've got a buddy list going on the Intranet, of people who have either experienced a physical or mental health condition or have a disability, as well as those with caring responsibilities. And all of the people involved are happy to be disclosed, and we connect people globally.

It began when we had someone in the office who was undergoing treatment for long-term illness. And while she said the support she received from the company was fantastic, she craved a connection with someone who had been in her shoes working on the ground, day to day, to advise her on certain practicalities that came with this illness. She found someone through brave conversation, and that inspired the start of the buddy list – in order to make fellow colleagues in similar situations easily available to help.

What can managers do to promote good mental health?

It's really important that line managers are really properly educated on the subject as it affects so many people. It's a real crusade of mine. We ran some line manager training sessions helping them to drive the conversation, break down the stigma and also recognise the signs and symptoms of mental health crisis.

I think the story-telling element is key: some of the most impactful sessions I've arranged or been to have been where people – junior and senior – have just talked about their personal experiences, because it brings the issues to life and people can relate to them.

Employee networks can also drive a huge amount of change. We are well-respected – we are fierce when we get going! – and people listen because they have such a huge amount of employee backing.

Chapter 8
SMART Working

Why the way we work is at the very heart of diversity and inclusion

In this section we look at:

- Why the concept of SMART Working has traditionally been an issue within the sector.
- The forces that are making employers reconsider their policies.
- How SMART working opens the workplace to a wider range of talent.
- How flexible working can be made to operate.
- The benefits to employers prepared to fully adopt flexible working.
- How the Covid crisis has demonstrated ways in which SMART Working can be rolled out, as well as highlighting some potential drawbacks.

The terms "SMART Working" and "flexible working" tend to be used interchangeably – and both are broadly applied to work patterns that allow employees to achieve a better work/life balance, as well as enabling employers to attract and/or retain talent that might otherwise be unavailable to them. This is particularly important for younger generations of employees but can also apply to older workers.

In many cases, having the option of flexible working is a decisive factor in a person being able to work at all because of other demands – such as care responsibilities, access issues or health considerations.

SMART Working is central to all of the different activity streams within the Diversity Project, simply because it enables so many people, who would otherwise be excluded from working in the investment and savings sector, to bring their talents to bear in the industry and to maximise their personal and professional potential.

There are three main factors to take on board when designing a flexible role: where, when and how the work is done, and the term can describe any kind of working pattern that doesn't fit into the traditional 9-5, five-day week and based in the employer's workplace – such as flexitime, part-time, working from home part or all of the week, annualized hours or compressing the working week into fewer days.

Because of SMART Working's pivotal role, in 2019, the Diversity Project and Timewise launched a collaborative effort to modernise working practices in the investment and savings industry. The aim was to deepen understanding around the cultural and operational barriers preventing more roles being open to flexible working, identify specific actions to overcome these and to test and share solutions.

The programme is supported by AXA Investment Managers, Aon, Fidelity International and St James's Place Wealth Management. The project is now moving into its support phase with core partners starting to implement recommendations with support from the Diversity Project and Timewise.

Critically, the contention of The Diversity Project and its partner, Timewise, is that flexible roles should be quality, permanent ones which benefit employers and employees alike, so this does not include zero-hours or temping contracts.

What the law says...

At present, even if you don't have flexible working written into your HR policies as standard practice, all employees can actually ask for it as individuals. That right was established in 2014 under the Flexible Working Regulations.

There are some caveats: the employee must have been working for the same employer for a minimum of 26 weeks, their request must be made in writing, and can only be made once a year. What's more, when they submit their application, the employee has to set out what effect they think it would have on the business.

Moreover, you, as an employer are entitled to say "no". But you are legally obliged to deal with any request "in a reasonable manner". This means properly considering the request, meeting the employee to discuss it and offering the possibility of an appeal if you turn their request down.

Of course, that is the default legal position: it's primarily reactive and places the onus on the employee. Even with that available to them, many employees in the investment and savings sector have shied away from applying their rights and asking for flexibility because of the perception that it would either not be granted or be seen as them displaying a lack of loyalty and/or ambition.

Many companies' HR policies on flexible working do, in fact, go further than the statutory minimum obligations. However, a common theme is that many employees, and even managers, aren't familiar with these policies.

The alternative approach for employers is to proactively take the opportunity to develop a company-wide HR strategy around flexibility that lets everyone know where they stand and acts as the starting point to developing ways of working within the company that actually make the most of the potential benefits of SMART working... and boosts their ability to attract and retain talent.

The impact of Covid-19

Since the Diversity Project launched their programme, the focus on flexible working has been hugely amplified by Covid-19. Across the globe, investment and savings firms have been forced – at pace and under pressure – to revise long-standing working practices and embrace remote working.

In the words of Helena Morrissey, Chair of the Diversity Project: "The real-life experience has demonstrated what was hard to prove in theory: that people can be at least as productive working from home as in the office and that almost every job in our industry can be performed remotely.

"It's broken the stigma attached to remote working in one fell swoop. Culturally, we had struggled to move away from 'presenteeism' – where hours at the (same) desk were viewed as a measure of commitment and performance. Now it's all about results. If we can build on these learnings, this is potentially a huge equalizer for men and women and a magnet for diverse talent."

As this book goes to press, business leaders across the globe are starting to realise that the initial response to implement remote working needs to be developed more strategically in order to make it a longer-term means of harnessing talent. Equally importantly, it has opened up the door to considering the other types of flexible working than remote working – not least, different working hours.

For the investment industry, one that has often struggled to modernise its working practices, this is an opportunity to improve both employee engagement and performance, attract diverse talent through new ways of working, and drive efficiencies and cost savings on office space.

Some supportive statistics

- 84% of men, 91% of women and 92% of millennials either work flexibly or wish they could.[22]
- 15% of current vacancies reference flexible working at the point of hire[23].
- Flexible working is considered highly important or essential for 77% of women, 80% of people with health concerns, 91% of carers and 74% of older workers.[24]
- 68% of organisations are taking steps to reduce stress and boost wellbeing in the workplace, of which 69% are using flexible working options to achieve this.[25]
- 63% of employees are more likely to stay with an employer who offers flexible working.[26]
- It costs an average of £30,000 to replace an employee.[27]
- 9 in 10 employees consider flexible working to be a key motivator to their productivity at work and 81% of

[22]White et al (2003) 'High-performance' Management Practices, Working Hours and Work–Life Balance
https://www.managers.org.uk/cmi-women/blueprint-for-balance; Berg et al., (2004); MacDermid & Tang, (2009)
[23] https://timewise.co.uk/article/flexible-jobs-index/
[24] "Addressing Barriers to Diversity in Portfolio Management: Performance & Continuity management" The Diversity Project
[25] "Financial Services Skills Taskforce: Final Report," 2020
[26] Working Lives Report Aviva 2017
[27] Working Lives Report Aviva 2017

those who have access to remote working believe it increases their productivity.[28]

- Deloitte, in their 2017 Millennial Survey,[29] found that in highly flexible working environments, only 2% more Millennial workers saw themselves leaving their job within two years rather than staying beyond five. In the least flexible organisations, the gap went up to 18%.

Ana Maria Tuliak

SMART Working workstream leader

I've worked with clients within the investments and savings industry for the last decade, and during that time, I have seen the diversity and inclusion agenda steadily advance as the benefits within firms become more apparent. Slowly but surely, there's been a growing realisation that SMART working is at the heart of making this happen - not just as an enabler for making workplaces more inclusive, but also making them more productive and more attractive.

---

[28]HSBC (2017) accessed at: https://www.about.hsbc.co.uk/-/media/uk/en/news.../171108-fl exible-working.pdf
[29]https://www2.deloitte.com/content/dam/Deloitte/global/Documents/About-Deloitte/gx-deloitte-millennial-survey-2017-executive-summary.pdf

Flexibility has traditionally been seen as a benefit for those who have served time or achieved seniority - not as a way to attract and retain top diverse talent. Now it is.

In part, that shift has been driven by market dynamics. After the last recession, complacency amongst employers in our industry was quite high. Employees, especially graduates, were happy just to have a job. As the market has recovered, D&I has risen up the agenda. "What works for the employee" has been talked about more openly as this is the key factor in (to apply a commonly used phrase in this context) "not just inviting people to come to the party, but to join in the dancing".

Covid-19 has massively accelerated that trend. Before then, in my experience, the majority of investment firms still valued presenteeism highly: being seen at your desk, the way it had always been done. Now, managers are having to change their metrics, and the post-Covid world will simply not be the same as the one before the lockdown.

The way remote working has been shown to work will give people throughout an organisation more confidence to ask for this and other forms of flexible working, both from their current employer and any future one.

Confidence to ask really is a key issue here, as I know from my own experience. Having worked for 6 ½ years in the industry, and not felt able to ask for more flexibility, I took a six months' sabbatical. When I came back, I reprioritised my life. I was no longer stuck in this bubble trying to work my way up the ladder. I felt able to assert that I would be more productive if I could work from home on Mondays to get on top of my strategy and plans for the week ahead. I have been working flexibly, location and hours-wise, ever since!

That was pre-Covid-19. Now, even though there's an economic crisis and a health crisis going on, we're still performing and still delivering the outcomes that we committed to.

Through the Diversity Project and my network of leaders within the industry, I and others have been lobbying firms to focus on outcomes as the main measure of productivity, rather than how many hours you've put in at the office. Yes, it's an important way to build relationships, but it's not a reliable measure just because it's a habitual cultural behaviour within a firm, and because people haven't challenged it.

The research undertaken by Timewise, which shows that 87% of job seekers in the UK are expecting some sort of flexibility[30], has been very visible with the candidates I work with. However, I see so many examples of there still

---

[30] https://timewise.co.uk/article/flexible-working-talent-imperative/

being a disconnect between what employees want and what some employers are prepared to provide.

Just before Covid-19, we were talking to an organisation whose perceived "flexibility" was to allow line managers to decide whether someone who asked could work from home for half a day a week – but only if they had a good reason, such as needing to be in to get their boiler fixed. This is a highly reactive rather than proactive approach: offering flexibility should be reason neutral, and part of your culture – not just a "benefit" within a manager's gift.

Another candidate came to us after they lost a parent: a challenging time for anyone. Even though their employer had a policy in place to support flexible working, they wouldn't allow that person to work flexibly to support their circumstances. They were so focussed on presenteeism that it eventually led to a parting of the ways.

Another candidate left their employer because – even though they were well aware that they were neurodivergent – they couldn't provide flexibility for them to attend hospital appointments.

How difficult will employers find it to switch from valuing presenteeism to quantifying outcomes?

Some will find it difficult because it's quite a big change in mentality, not just in working practices. All our experience shows that the firms that have done well with this have embedded flexibility within their core values and brought all of their managers on board to understand, appreciate and implement it.

Conversely, many companies will tell you that they already have flexible working enshrined in their company policies... but the reality is somewhat different. I know of one company which had a flexible working policy in place for over 20 years, but no one had ever worked flexibly for them. The prevailing culture of presenteeism hadn't supported it. And everyone has been too scared to do it first because of that.

Within that firm, it was only after one of their star fund managers role-modelled working out of the office that it slowly began to gain acceptance – starting with more senior personnel. But a lot of communication had to be done internally to get to the point where the culture came across as acceptable and supportive of this.

It has to come from the top: all too often, you have "group-think" within the boardroom, and they then don't support the middle and line managers. Managers must have the right training support and the right tools to create and nurture a flexible working environment.

Making the business case count

We've been doing a lot of work on building the business case for SMART or flexible working, because these are the messages that will cut through to a lot of people. Fortunately, there's multiple research and backing data to demonstrate that – without it – you won't be able to attract and retain a diverse workforce, affecting your business prospects long term.

What's more, as well as bullet-proofing your business for the future, you are also working on your ESG (Environmental, Social & Corporate Governance) and being seen to act in the interests of the broader stakeholders of society.

In addition, firms need to be aware that generational forces will also soon start to shift the argument, as more Millennials enter the boardroom and the old ways of thinking are replaced and the barriers overcome.

What other arguments need to be won?

A lot of firms say, "Oh, we'd love to try it – but the regulatory system doesn't allow it. Fund managers cannot work remotely." The contention is that fund managers working out of another location present an increased risk of insider trading.

This is a myth, but it has persisted – and acted as a deterrent. Many fund managers already work flexibly, and it functions very well. The regulators, the FCA, have never said that flexible working is not supported by them...

There is a huge gap between the 83% of people wanting flexibility at the point of hire and the 10% of jobs that are openly advertised within asset management as "flexible". A lot of employers say to me: "We'll be flexible for the right person." But when they come to choose between two candidates, they'll go with the safe option because that is what they know.

Part of my work is to challenge these old ways of working, and thinking, and letting employers clearly understand that the top talent now requires this.

Emma Stewart

CEO and Co-Founder of Timewise, which partners the Diversity Project's SMART Working workstream.

I'd describe Timewise as a social business with a mission to get everybody the flexibility they need in the workplace... without compromising their careers.

My own life experience and the barriers I met in my career have gone into Timewise: I set the business up in 2005 because I fell out of work as a senior TV producer after having children.

Timewise undertakes a lot of research, thought leadership, and campaign work to champion the benefits of flexibility, and also provides consultancy and training for employers who want to get better at flexible working. We also run our own job site for candidates who are returning to work, or who have negotiated more flexibility in the job they're in and can't find any jobs they can apply for that will give them the same flexibility.

How much of a problem is flexible working for the industry?

We run a national index each year tracking the vacancy market, and only 15% of job advertisements mention any form of flexibility[31] – so 85% of six million job vacancies say nothing at all about an organisation's openness to having a conversation about flexibility.

And yet, research carried out in 2020 shows that, following Covid, nine out of ten people in the workforce now want to work flexibly[32].

Many people are now working flexibly because they have negotiated it with their employer, and of course, they want it in their next job. So, what happens? They look at job ads that don't mention flexibility and don't apply for them. Or there's a "game of chicken" when they apply and wonder when to ask about it: when they apply, in the interview, or

[31] https://timewise.co.uk/article/flexible-jobs-index/
[32] https://workplaceinsight.net/large-majority-of-people-want-to-continue-some-form-of-flexible-working/

after they are offered the job? The onus is all on the candidate.

The bottom line is that there are really good people who won't be applying for certain jobs because they are not confident enough to have that conversation.

How does the sector compare in its approach to flexibility?

While there has been some openness to flexible working, there hasn't really been that much good practice in the context of advertising jobs as flexible at the point of hire. And when you get into a conversation around management practice and capability, it maybe hasn't gone so deep as some of the other professional service firms.

Internationally, if you look west, we compare relatively favourably with the States, where we know there are still some real challenges, especially related to workers' rights.

If we look to Europe, there are some really interesting lessons that we can learn, particularly from the Scandinavian countries, where people are encouraged to balance work and care more effectively. We probably sit between the two.

For instance, only 7% of workers in our sector work part-time (compared to a UK average of 28%)[33]. This was why, in 2020, The Diversity Project and Timewise launched a joint project with support from four founding partners to dig under the skin of why there are barriers to improving flexible working within the industry, and to try and understand what are the constraints... are they operationally real or simply perceived because of fixed mindsets and company cultures?

Our main concern is that it's currently all very reactive. Individuals at a senior level are able to negotiate and get what they want because they are very highly valued. Those new to the industry or in more junior roles don't feel they can necessarily ask — certainly not without impacting on their career progression.

So, there's a non-conversation happening.

There are a number of risks that we see, which affect people in different ways and predominantly affect women more. You ask to go part-time, and the employer says yes - but the job isn't really redesigned to reflect that. You're still expected to produce the same outputs. The answer to that is to support managers to redesign jobs differently if

---

[33]https://diversityproject.com/2020-05-12/why-our-savings-and-investments-project-more-critical-now-ever

someone goes part-time, as well as work out how to get the additional output out of somebody else.

"Returners" present another cause for concern. They leave because they can't balance work and care, so the best way to attract them back into organisations should be to give them the flexibility they need. Businesses keen to attract returners will set up returner programmes, focussed around coaching and getting people back up to speed. But all too often, the job itself isn't flexible; or, if it is, they haven't redesigned the outputs and expectations for it being part-time.

What, then, is the solution?

A far more effective solution, we believe, is changing your recruitment processes: advertise all your roles as flexible and you will attract those returners – and more. And you can always provide some intensive coaching for anyone who may require it after a long career break.

Managers also need to be supported to really understand the nature of each job and what the expectations should be in terms of output. Historically, it may have been about someone working 45 hours a week; turn that on its head and instead break the job down into tasks and activities and understand how much of their time they will spend delivering these objectives. Critically, if you are going to have a conversation with someone about doing 80% of that role, which activities do you take out?

Also, to be factored in is that we all function at different levels: some people may be able to perform more intensively than others. Therefore, it's about understanding what your expectations are in terms of outputs and performance from an individual within a role, and then adjusting that if you want to change the hours.

If you get performance right, and you understand the nature of job design, you can work out how to divide jobs up much more effectively.

Because we're currently in this request/response mode, where an individual has to ask to work less, there's a responsibility on both sides to think of the effect on the team: if you are taking five hours out of a job, where do those five hours go? Do they get dispersed amongst the rest of the team; in which case, are they happy with that? Do they not get done because, actually, you can afford to lose that activity? Do they get done as the person performs more efficiently… because they're working from home and not getting bothered by lots of phone calls? Or do you need to find somebody else in that team to pick up those five hours?

That's the reason why we have these conversations about "floodgates": managers are rightly worried that you can get to a tipping point: you have five people in your team and everybody wants to work 0.8 - and there's a whole job that you've lost. But as long as you can face up to that, you can think about resourcing things differently.

Managers also need to work with Finance to have the freedom and flexibility to do this: we need to start thinking more creatively about how to measure on FTE rather than headcount. If you have ten people in your team rather than seven because you've got three people job sharing, that may be costing you a little bit more… but you'll be delivering far more output as a result.

Valuing part-time workers

The evidence shows that the main driver for the gender pay gap is women choosing to work part-time, and women are less likely to be promoted when they work part-time. Behind that is an inherent assumption that, because they are working part-time, they are less committed, and therefore, of less value. So, it's a circle…

But there are some deeper issues. Unless you redesign expectations for part-time workers, they often get measured on the same metrics as full-time workers, with the risk that they are recorded as being less productive and effective. That means that as well as being seen as "not committed 100% to my business", they are also perceived as not performing as well.

The fact that, increasingly, men are asking to go part-time for a better work/life balance or to share care responsibilities, offers the hope that – eventually – this will be less of a gender issue. We know from research that many younger men would choose flexibility over remuneration in their next job.

This should wake business leaders up to the fact that this really is a talent issue: if you don't get this right, you should be worried that you will start to lose men from your business as well as women.

However, even in this current crisis, there is evidence that in dual-income households which are having to deal with home schooling and balancing life and work, working women currently spend an average of 15 hours a week more on unpaid domestic labour than men[34].

What women need is for more men to be living and feeling that experience.

And it's not just about caring for kids. Older people also have major caring responsibilities – and around one in three people in the workforce are aged 50 and over.[35]

---

[34]https://www.bbc.com/worklife/article/20200630-how-covid-19-is-changing-womens-lives
[35]https://www.bitc.org.uk/age-and-multigeneration-teams/

The Covid crisis has shone a very harsh light on our institutional framework that allows people to work and care. Take away schools, nurseries, and various forms of social care, and you realise that we need all this infrastructure in order to work. We must recognise that, in business, we are only able to get people to work if they are able to fit work around everything else that's going on in their lives, and that we will get much more out of them if we can help them get that balance right.

Is progress being made?

The fact that, increasingly, businesses are coming to us to ask for advice and support shows progress. When we started 15 years ago, we didn't have a lot of the legislation that we have in place today. Flexibility has now landed.

We show a "maturity curve" in our presentations which illustrates the journey of how businesses can go from being inherently "reactive" – and giving permission to the odd person to work flexibly – through to being systemically "flexible". The companies coming to us for advice recognise that they are still near the start of the journey and that they need to work at it. And that's an important message. You don't just change behaviour and culture overnight. You don't just tell a manager to design a job differently and it happens. Or expect a manager to suddenly manage a dispersed team of 25 people that they don't see from day to day.

That requires vision, principles and a big shift from simply having a flexible working policy to actually having a strategy. Because this is about organisational design. And it's about behaviour.

Sometimes, businesses don't act because they're worried about not being able to have a one-size-fits-all solution across all teams and disciplines, and that doesn't feel fair. But there's a big difference between equality and fairness, and if you can shift the culture to one where it is proactive rather than reactive and encourage teams to talk about how they are working, you can start to flesh out and assuage some of those anxieties.

We run training sessions for middle managers, and, when they are given the forum to think and talk about making it work, they often come up with the solutions themselves. It's about businesses giving managers permission to try different things – particularly at the point of hire.

Headhunters and recruitment agencies can play a role in changing company attitudes – and many are starting to do that – but it's fundamentally the responsibility of the business to be open to that conversation.

That is our big, big message. If you want to get great people into your business, why are you not having this conversation about flexibility with your candidates, in the same way as you would with people already in your organisation?

What can YOU do to be a SMART Working company?

Informed by the findings from their research, the Diversity Project has published a SMART Working Manifesto for Change which presents a challenge to the investment and savings industry to ensure flexible working is encouraged and developed more strategically.

In it, they call out to firms to commit to five actions for a more sustainable approach to flexible working:

1. **Leaders will lead and model inclusive cultures and behaviours**: *CEOs and leaders must be seen to champion flexible working to set the vision and cultural tone of the organisation. Executives must make it a strategic issue for the whole organisation, and not an issue that is solely for HR to address.*

2. **Flexible working arrangements will be reason neutral**: *Internal communication and organisational culture will support conversations with both men and women at all levels on HOW not WHY flexible working should be facilitated.*

3. **Flexibility will be designed into jobs as standard**: *Hiring managers will be encouraged to consider whether job vacancies can be open to flexible working at the point of hire and, if so, make a clear statement to that effect to candidates, both internal and external.*

4. **Managers will be supported to build their capabilities to manage flexible and dispersed teams**: *Firms need to invest in providing training to managers as part of L&D to enable them to build the knowledge and skills to manage flexible teams in an inclusive, reason neutral way and build skills for flexible job design in order to adjust working patterns at a team level.*

5. **Managers should take a proactive approach to reviewing flexible working arrangements**: *All recovery and "return to work" pulse surveys and conversations post-Covid 19 should be proactively addressed and include the option for employees to retain some form of flexible working.*

Chapter 9
Harnessing the data

... or why data is the key to achieving greater diversity

Making substantive progress in all of the streams discussed in this book depends upon a series of factors: not least, changing cultures, changing practices and changing attitudes. But unless we have a firm grasp of who is currently working in the industry, we have no way of knowing how far we have to travel... or when we get there.

Jo Livermore

Diversity Project workstream leader

I've been in HR generalist roles for 21 years and I come at this from several angles: firstly, as an HR professional; and, secondly, as an employer. Through the Diversity Project, I'm also engaged with a network of HR professionals looking at the issues and sharing the challenges.

Previous to asset management, I worked for an insurance company, in the legal industry and in retail banking. My prior experience tells me that there needn't be an issue around data in asset management.

When I worked in insurance (starting 20 years ago), we were collecting diversity data then. All the excuses and obstacles within the Asset Management sector are very interesting to me, given that other sectors are handling this perfectly well and without controversy.

The issues we have in the sector are primarily down to concerns around reputation: as an Asset Manager, your reputation is crucial in terms of legal and regulatory exposure. And, in Asset Management, regulation is fairly new, whereas other industries are very used to it. I think that "newness" is what scares people sometimes.

The flip side of reputation, however, is that if you don't have a diverse workforce, and you're not doing all you can to create a culture of inclusivity, then that is potentially damaging – and that is what the industry is waking up to now.

Collecting data can be quite a manual process, and therefore, an investment in technology is probably required in order to do this properly. That is not always undertaken by companies, but that should not be a barrier.

Privacy will – understandably - be uppermost in many people's minds, and GDPR has added a different flavour to things. But we've always had privacy laws; it's always been illegal to mismanage data; GDPR has simply upped the ante. All GDPR did was say, "This is how much you'll get fined if you don't get this right".

The other common concern is the employment law angle: using data in a discriminatory way. That said, these are obstacles that can be overcome... and are overcome in other industries. So, to me, it's quite baffling how the Asset Management sector continues to make excuses for not collecting the data in the first place. Moreover, the raw set of data tells you nothing. You need to bring in other data points to make it meaningful: promotions tracking, the pay gap and so on. Then, you can meaningfully track the trends over time.

However, how we use - or don't use - the data does require some discretion. If, for instance, I have just one black fund manager, and I present data at too granular a level, you can identify that person, their earnings and so on... and that's why people can get protective. Yes, there is a tension here but that shouldn't stop us from pushing forwards. I'm saying to my leaders at the moment: "You can see what's around you. Unless we get on with solving the problem that we know we have, we're kicking the can down the road."

The other thing that Asset Managers need to do is use the data to establish targets: to disclose to the internal and external world, this is our current demographic, and this is where we want to get to. You are effectively saying: "Yes, we know it's not great at present, but we are demonstrating that we know there's a problem, and we are committed to monitoring progress and making improvements."

And making improvements will be essential: we're fairly hypocritical because, when we invest, we measure the quality of a firm in terms of their credentials around diversity, leadership effectiveness and capability, and yet many of us do not demonstrate this in our own organisations.

What can Asset Management learn from other sectors' experience?

Insurance, for instance, has more client-facing roles and a faster turnover of staff. They have had to work hard at this stuff to retain talent. I appreciate that Asset Management is a longer game: people tend to remain longer, which is one of the reasons you don't get the diversity in the industry and the opportunity to keep the diversity dial moving.

But what you can learn from the Insurance industry is their greater employee engagement and inclusivity, and the fact that theirs is an environment where people are comfortable with disclosing their data because they know you're going to do something useful with it. Their leaders are also managing a more complex and diverse workforce – younger, more demanding in what they expect. Asset Management is only just starting to experience that groundswell from within, but at some point, that is where we will be.

How do you strike the balance between confidentiality and transparency?

That is the real challenge for firms. But for me, that's a problem that we've made up for ourselves. For instance, I have not experienced a situation where an employee has raised a grievance or taken their firm to a tribunal because they didn't trust the way their firm was handling their data. It's the actions taken as a result of gathering the data that is the important part of the piece – and what we are continuing to grapple with... otherwise, we would have been putting action into place already.

The industry is made up of people who don't see that there's a problem because they've done very well out of the situation. It's a low turnover industry, so we have to take affirmative action if we are going to change it – and that, in itself, poses challenges if we want to avoid "tokenism" and to get the very best person for the job.

As HR people, the way we achieve that is by ensuring that our initial long and short-listed candidate lists are as diverse as they can be. Then you have to measure the candidates by whatever criteria you have for that role.

If you only turn down a white guy because he's a white guy then you've strayed into the same territory as if you'd turned down a Black person because they were Black. You've got to focus on capabilities. You've got to focus on competencies. And you've just to make sure that the candidate list is as diverse as it can be from the outset.

How diverse is the talent pool when you do look to recruit?

We know we need to fill the industry from the bottom up, but that's going to take us 15 or 20 years. So, at the moment in our business, we are focusing on our early careers programme to make sure we get that pipeline coming through. But when we're looking for experienced hires, it's hard. The diverse pool is not so readily available. That's when we challenge ourselves: is a specific type of experience or competency essential, or could we hire differently?

It can take longer if you're determined to hire someone from a diverse background, and you'll probably have to pay more to attract talent away from another firm. Moreover, you have to find very robust reasons for turning down the typical candidates who will be applying for that role – who are very experienced, very capable and tick all the boxes.

That's a real challenge and, within my own firm, we're working with our search firm to do just that.

Internally, we are also debating on where you compromise on specific experience, accepting that a diverse candidate may bring something else to the party... something we never knew we needed but actually, when we think about it, we could use within the firm. And that comes back to the whole reason why you would have a diverse candidate in the first place: you have to look at what value they can add to your firm that perhaps you didn't realise you needed.

Could that mean recruiting from outside your industry?

Exactly. But then you've got to have leaders capable of on-boarding and inducting that person – because these candidates will inevitably not look and act the same as every-body else – as well as create an environment where they will be comfortable. Once you've found that candidate, you also need to accept that they are going to take longer to get up to speed, while people around them are asking: "Why did you hire them?"

This is a whole new skill set that people in the industry will need to learn.

Moreover, with the introduction of SM&CR, the regulator doesn't like it if you have a vacancy there for too long... but the regulator is also driving greater diversity in the indus-try. In fact, the FCA came out recently saying that if you continue, as an industry, to try and register the same folks in these same leadership roles in senior management functions, then they're going to challenge that, because they're not seeing enough diversity in the industry. It's a real push and pull.

Should the data be used to create "league tables"?

I would endorse publishing the data that shows which companies are doing well on diversity because it does hold you to account. That said, the gender pay gap hasn't driven change yet, partly, at least, because it's so systemic.

What I'm trying to get our leaders to focus on is creating a culture of inclusivity for everybody: rather than focus on making sure you have the right number of people with certain characteristics, create a culture of inclusivity through the procedures and practices you have in place: then you attract and retain the talent.

One of the happy outcomes of Covid is the flexible working environment that we now all work in, and that's an advantage to parents and carers, whichever way they self-identify from a diversity perspective. It has also meant that we have been more deliberate in our communication with employees, more collaborative, we've had to work differently as teams. And that will benefit all individuals, regardless of how they identify.

How can leaders best work with their HR teams to achieve greater diversity?

My impression from having conversations with my HR network is that HR continues to get the blame for the issues. And we are in a tricky situation. We are obliged to protect our organisations from legal action, and we're obliged to protect employees from unfair treatment.

At the same time, we are being asked to be affirmative with our actions. But it's not us that needs to do that. It's the leaders who need to think differently and drive a different culture. We are obliged to train them in that and help with their development and their capabilities. HR teams tend to be reactive rather than proactive.

The other complexity that I and other of my HR colleagues are navigating is globalisation. Many of my peers work for non-UK-headquartered asset managers, so parent companies can be working within different jurisdictions, with different risk appetites and exposures. The strive to have global consistency within an organisation often derails or slows down action.

You can't possibly have consistency within D&I across a global business because you are operating in totally different geographies and cultures.

Chapter 10
The Asset Owners perspective

So far in this book, I've examined the issue of diversity from the perspective of groups seeking greater inclusivity within the investments and savings sector, as well as looked at the benefits to the industry of taking that on board. One final very important perspective remains: that is of the industry's clients – pension funds, institutional investors, family offices and retail investors... the asset owners.

Helen Price

Asset Owners' Workstream

Asset owners invariably make clear to stakeholders their commitment to diversity and they, in turn, can wield significant influence to ensure the companies managing their assets are equally committed.

That's why the Diversity Project workstream is so relevant; it explores barriers to entry, retention, and promotion for asset managers from different backgrounds.

At Brunel Pension Partnership, I lead on stewardship, engagement, and voting, and so have direct experience of how this can work. Our approach is to routinely ask asset managers about diversity within their companies as part of ongoing monitoring, but it's difficult to ascertain what "good" actually looks like.

It's easy enough for a company to give us their policy, tell us they've got employee groups, and assure us they think diversity is important. But what does it all actually mean? Conversely, it's really difficult for asset owners to assess whether diversity and inclusion (D&I) are embedded appropriately or not, and whether the theme is being taken seriously.

Making comparisons between different companies, or setting up league tables, is also problematic because an international business will have different policies for each territory. There will be differences between various industry areas. And that's before you start to think about the size of the asset manager. For example, within a larger company employing more staff, each member represents a small percentage of the population – and vice versa in a small company.

Also, if you have one company with a lower starting point, they could consistently be at the bottom of the diversity rankings, even though they are making progress vs a company which had less to do. And it can be difficult to compare when you have varying level of diversity at different levels within a company. Quantitative information can be really useful as a signal to have a conversation, but you also need the qualitative story for the whole picture.

All that said, in general terms, I'd say that the situation is improving across the asset management industry. One of the great strengths of the Diversity Project is that we are able to speak candidly to individuals who are passionate about inclusion and diversity from a range of different companies and find out from them the challenges they are facing and how they are tackling them. Historically, there was not a lot of public information. You wouldn't see it on their website, and it was hard to tell from the outside what the industry baseline was.

The Diversity Project gives you access to what some of those policies might be.

The Project also gives us access to information that we can feedback internally, enabling us to look at ourselves: how we are handling diversity and what improvements we can make. It's about sharing best practice or sharing challenges and solutions.

For example, one discussion held within the asset managers group is around the change in how you certify people within the industry. Now, we have moved to the senior management certification regime (SMCR), there are questions over, for example, whether someone who's away for 12 weeks is still classified as a certified person. Asset managers are interpreting that in different ways – especially around maternity, enhanced paternity or shared parental leave. Some say you've been away and need to be recertified; others say that, since you've always been here, you don't need anything new.

As a result of this issue being flagged up, individuals within the group went back to their compliance teams and were able to share the approaches they were taking. Moreover, the group raised this with the Financial Conduct Authority (FCA) as a potential issue. It certainly is not the intention of the FCA to create any barriers to diversity, and the group has asked us to go out and find more information and let the FCA know how it is being interpreted to see if there is anything further that the FCA may need to do.

How do you separate those that are polishing their policies for your benefit from those actually making cultural change?

Within our firm, there will be initial questions within the tender exercise, and you can see quite quickly whether they have policies in place. With those that don't, it's normally a signal that it's not something that they are looking at.

Then, when we take the asset manager through to the next stages, we do due diligence and question them a lot more on the detail. For instance: whether they have information around KPIs; whether they have tied it into remuneration of employees; and who's got ownership: the board and partners, or those lower down, such as middle managers?

That level of information can give you an indication of how seriously they are taking it.

How committed, for instance, are they to things like the Women in Finance Charter[36], and the more recent Race at Work Charter[37]? These are good, constructive initiatives because, if you sign up to a charter, you have to set targets and annually disclose your performance against them. Some of the more progressive asset managers (I'm not saying all of them!) tend to be signed up to these initiatives as well as to initiatives such as the Diversity Project and 30% Club[38]. But there are other questions worth asking, too.

Are they working with organisations like Investment 2020?[39] Or targeting specific groups for internships? What are they doing to improve the perception of the industry? How many of their staff have actually taken up enhanced leave; how many have returned; and do they know how

---

[36] https://www.gov.uk/government/publications/women-in-finance-charter
[37] https://www.bitc.org.uk/wp-content/uploads/2019/10/bitc-race-report-raceatworkchartersurveyoneyearoncasestudies-oct2019.pdf
[38] https://30percentclub.org/
[39] https://www.investment2020.org.uk/

long their staff stay for after they've been on leave? Is there enough support in place for returning staff?

Digging deeper at the due diligence stage means you soon get to the bottom of whether or not policies are being followed through.

Are you pushing at an open door or meeting resistance around diversity?

The door is certainly more open than it was before: specifically, it's easier to have conversations around gender diversity. However, you still sometimes hear: "We've put one female on the board, now stop talking about it…"

But diversity is a continually evolving theme.

Over the last year, I've seen more asset managers realise that this could actually be a very useful thing for them. We've seen the launch of investments specifically targeted at diversity; the launch of indices that target diversity; and of impact funds as well, including some that support women in less developed countries.

However, we do still get push back – most often from the US – and here it comes down to a legal and data-sharing perspective. Why are you asking for this information and what are you going to do with it? There is concern around data privacy, yes, but also over where we are going to compare them with other asset managers.

However, there are ways in which data can be shared in line with the law, safely and in pursuit of a common goal.

We are seeing improvements. ISS (Institutional Shareholder Services[40]) wrote to the FTSE 100 and S&P over the summer[41] asking for greater disclosure around ethnicity data and other diversity metrics, and they've seen some improvements. That information is now being fed back. ISS, though, is a paid-for resource, and I do question whether diversity data should be a paid-for resource, as it could slow progress.

What would progress over the next couple of years look like to you?

Greater disclosure from asset managers, and for them to be taking a lead in providing that.

Also, having more asset owners as part of the Diversity Project. I'm actually working with a group of asset owners at the moment, and the idea is for an asset owners' working group to develop a pledge or charter, with the objective of formalising a set of actions that asset owners can commit to in order to improve diversity, in all forms, across the investment industry. This would focus on three key aspects:

---

[40] https://www.issgovernance.com/
[41] https://www.ft.com/content/b45f6a13-c8e6-484b-a75f-bb578178e87f

- Embedding diversity & inclusion questions into the tender process, ensuring it forms part of the scored criteria
- Embedding it into the investment management agreement and annual manager monitoring
- And then walking the walk – and part of this will be working with industry bodies

The hope is that the three key aspects would lead to a more consistent and common approach across the asset management industry. Often, there is pressure to consolidate D&I questions during the tender process, and so the group is developing a questionnaire, which will enable a range of questions to be asked during ongoing manager monitoring. We're also working with other groups in this field with the hope that, within a year, we can pull all of this data together and create a report, assessing where we are. That would enable asset owners to look at managers and determine whether or not they want to consider them as part of a tender assessment.

If we can do this, it would send a clear, strong message that asset owners take diversity seriously.

How is the Diversity Project helping to effect change?

From our perspective, the benefit of the Diversity Project is the shared, open dialogue that enables people to talk about the challenges – even, for instance, how they can talk about the topic to their management. It's just a great way to learn from one another and discover what best practice looks like. It means finding out what has worked and what hasn't.

One example is the #IAM[42] "TalkAboutBlack" movement that went viral over the summer, in the wake of Black Lives Matter. Before that, ethnic diversity was often a topic that people felt uncomfortable raising – not because they didn't want to, but because they were often afraid of using the wrong language or being misinterpreted. The way the campaign was framed, and not politicised, allowed people to just talk about race – not necessarily about the things that happened but around the root causes of racial ine-quality – it removed barriers. The work that has emerged from this movement is remarkable – for example, the 10,000 Black intern's initiative - and I'm hopeful the mo-mentum continues.

One of the things you often get with the asset manage-ment industry when you're asking about diversity is that managers say they "measure diversity of thought" within a workforce that is predominantly male, white, and mid-dle-aged... "We've done these assessments and we've got great diversity of thought: so-and-so spent two weeks in SE Asia." You need to be sure that going down the

[42]https://diversityproject.com/events/2020/join-movement-iamtalkingabout black

"diversity of thought" route doesn't mean that you ignore diversity of ethnicity, gender, background and so on.

If you're not contributing to that, you are part of the prob-lem.

Chapter 11
Build Back Better

"This pandemic has forced a change momentum upon us; now is the opportunity to accelerate positive change. With such an uncertain outlook, it is more important than ever to embrace inclusivity and diversity to enable business resilience and to build back better. This is true for any industry, but the focus on ESG investing makes it vital for our industries' credibility and legitimacy."

Jayne Styles

Co-Lead Diversity Project - Ambassador Programme

This book was written in the throes of a worldwide pandemic; and, while that has directly influenced many sections, it is well worth focussing on the longer-term ramifications of COVID-19 for diversity and inclusion.

In July 2020, the Diversity Project published a paper entitled "The Build Back Better Diversity Project"[43] written by Jayne Styles. Like institutions and businesses around the world – as well as many individuals – members of the Diversity Project recognise that positives can, and should, be

---

[43] https://diversityproject.com/resource/build-back-better

drawn out of what has been a tumultuous and damaging year in so many ways.

As the paper's preface makes clear: "Whilst the outlook remains unclear and businesses face many challenges, there are also real opportunities to reshape the future and for the investment industry to emerge stronger, more resilient, and modernised.

"Rapid change has already happened, and people are expecting more, so let us seize this moment. Inclusivity and diversity are enablers to building back better. With a strong sense that feelings of corporate inclusion have risen during the crisis, we need to leverage this momentum, as there is still a long way to go."

A life-threatening pandemic has forced society to work in very different ways than ever before as well as to re-evaluate many of its priorities. What, then, might an investment and savings sector built back in a better way look like? And what are the key components to achieving that? Importantly, how should business leaders shape their strategies as national lockdown periods ease whilst also ensuring the fight for equality is not lost?

My approach is to look at it through the lens of "ambidextrous leadership" – loosely defined as simultaneously harnessing explorative and exploitative approaches, where exploration embraces experimentation and innovation, whilst exploitation focuses on refinement and implementation.

An ambidextrous leadership approach can assist in supporting many of the paper's recommendations as they are complex... and potentially paradoxical. Moreover, with COVID-19 comes a chance to radicalise our efforts to avoid conscious or unconscious discriminatory habits and behaviours, but history tells us that we have a habit of returning to old behaviours in times of crisis.

Many businesses will be under severe financial pressures - not always the ideal setting for advancing cultural shifts which are seen as long-term investments. Already, in some parts of the economy, we are seeing echoes from the more recent financial crash of 2008 where businesses adopted extensive cost-saving activities in their efforts to survive, and which (arguably) led, in the main, to draconian HR practices such as compulsory redundancies, simplification of contracts, outsourcing and de-skilling of workforces.

Building Back Better: the recommendations

In light of the challenges faced by the sector, the report focuses on four key areas through the diversity and inclusion lens: Working location, Wellbeing, Culture and Flexibility.

Working location

Many workers have welcomed working from home and have largely come to terms with the "new normal" of flexible working – including video-calling and conferencing – and the financial sector has rapidly adapted. However, while it has enabled many to combine care duties, achieve a better work/life balance or reduce the hours they commute, it has not suited those employees whose circumstances are not well suited to remote working, and who have found the situation stressful and often isolating.

The report highlights that the post-lockdown return to work requires careful planning, but potential cost savings of building more remote working into a company's HR strategy could include reducing workspace allocations for employees and closing or shrinking expensive national offices in favour of regional hubs.

Critically, a new blended approach to working locations requires employers to consider the implications for all groups of employees and how they support this changing environment.

For instance, employers need to encourage staff to agree a daily agenda with their partners that allows childcare shifts to be arranged around work, and times of the day, identified with their manager, when an employee is not available, with managers focusing on productivity rather than the number of hours worked.

Similarly, older workers may have caring responsibilities (and require a similar flexible approach to their work patterns and management).

Roberts and McCluney 2020[44] highlights that working from home provides an additional challenge for Black employees, who regularly manage their professional image by code-switching. The video-calling technology widely used during lockdown removes Black employees' choice about how they present themselves and sends social messages about their home environments. To address this issue, employers need to encourage the social norm of video backgrounds and flexibility to have cameras off during larger meetings.

Wellbeing

During the crisis, the well-established office environment and routines have been replaced by the isolation of home working; and, although working from home may have had a positive effect on their productivity and sleep, it has increased anxiety over the pandemic and impacted

---

[44]Working from Home While Black *Harvard Business Review* [Online]. [Accessed 28 July 2020].

employees' stress levels around safety, control and human connection.

This has led many employers to actively publicise their employee assistance schemes, mental health first-aiders and schedule company wide self-care days.

These are measures that need to continue in the post-COVID world. Moreover, employers should be particularly aware, when planning their wellbeing strategy, of considering specific support for younger workers and women.

Social relationships at work are a major source of job satisfaction and social support, losing these has been a significant negative for many employees. Moreover, the issues can be exaggerated for younger employees – as highlighted in research into the experience of younger employees working from home by Klopotek (2017)[45], which identifies difficulty in separating home affairs from the professional ones and social isolation as key wellbeing issues for this group.

To support this group, employers need to establish and nurture virtual social networks, buddy schemes and virtual

---

[45]The Advantages and Disadvantages of Working Remotely from the Perspective of Young Employees. *Organization & Management Quarterly,* 40, 39-49.

"let's talk" sessions to encourage colleagues to share tips that are helping them deal with issues.

Women have been disproportionally impacted by the stresses of juggling multiple competing demands during lockdown. Research carried out during the lockdown period by Campbell (2020)[46] highlights that female parents are spending seven hours in an average weekday on childcare, compared with five hours for male parents – in part, at least, perhaps explaining that, during lockdown, 53% of women have felt more anxious and depressed than usual.

Employers need to consider providing informal time off, encourage people to take short breaks, such as an afternoon every week or a full day here and there for family time, with managers respecting this time off.

Culture

The report identifies the fact that during the lockdown period, empathy within companies has increased and corporate cultures have become more inclusive; and, as a result, employee's expectations have risen - meaning that a return to the older ways of doing things will be problematic to staff morale and loyalty as well as a loss to the companies themselves.

---

[46]*Women doing more childcare under lockdown but men more likely to feel their jobs are suffering* [Online]. London: Kings College London.

This leads directly to the Diversity and Inclusion agenda, and the report argues that challenges of a competitive environment are best met by a diverse workforce and an inclusive culture – and that companies should:

1. Commit to diversity and inclusion by aligning values, executive support and signing up for charters that require action.
2. Role model through executive behaviour, storytelling, normalising flexible working and committing to inclusive leadership by being compassionate, kind and curious about staff.
3. Implement visible, well-funded diversity and inclusion strategies with KPIs measuring collective and individual performance.

Flexibility

In its final chapter, the report identifies that the COVID crisis has helped break down historic resistance within the industry from line managers by proving that companies can operate remotely – and there is now a need to emphasise the positives of this experience and reinforce that this is now the norm.

However, there is still a need to take simple "working from home" further – and make the workplace truly flexible. The

Diversity Project's own manifesto for change (Tuliak and Stewart, 2020)[47] proposes five key actions to achieve this:

1. CEOs must be seen to champion flexible working, to set the vision and cultural tone of the organisation.
2. Flexible working arrangements will be reason neutral.
3. Flexibility will be designed into jobs as standard.
4. Managers will be supported to build their capabilities to manage flexible and dispersed teams.
5. Managers should take a proactive approach to reviewing flexible working arrangements.

---

[47]https://diversityproject.com/resource/smart-working-manifesto-change-investment-and-saving-industry

Chapter 12
Call to Action

The Diversity Project has remained true to its original template as an agile organisation relying on people voluntarily assuming roles to press forward agendas they are passionate about. Front and centre of the progress made to date has been the marketing strategy driven by Linda Russheim, who, through the Project's ever-expanding website, social media channels, series of publications, e-newsletters, webinars and events as well as working with Lansons, the Diversity Project's pro-bono PR agency, has ensured that the benefits of diversity and inclusion reach an ever-increasing audience.

Linda Russheim

Diversity Project Marketing

What are the messages at the heart of the Diversity Project marketing strategy?

The importance of cognitive diversity is the message that ties all the work across the Diversity Project together and has the benefit of resonating with the widest population. When we focus on the importance of having great talent and different perspectives, we get great engagement. I would say that our messaging has evolved as the Project has evolved.

Underneath cognitive diversity, the benefit is that each key group of stakeholders - asset owners, asset managers or consultants - can all find something that works for them. And that also works across the different aspects of diversity.

How much persuading do companies need that this is important?

This varies from organisation to organisation depending on where they are on their D&I journey. So, some more than others, and there are also different triggers for the various audiences we're talking to.

If we're talking to the CEOs of our Members, the mention of P&Ls definitely gets their attention. For others, the focus is more about culture and the concept of belonging, or just the right thing to do. If you look at the Diversity Project's manifesto, it's primary focus is that we should get more diverse talent into the industry to ensure that you are doing the best for your clients, and that you are staying relevant, resilient and don't get disrupted.

It is changing though, and Covid has accelerated that; but, at the end of the day, it still feels essentially P&L related.

How do you determine your marketing priorities?

The scope has extended well beyond what we originally talked about: I never imagined we'd end up with 17 workstreams! At the beginning of each year, we try to determine what is going to be important and set a plan for the year. We also recognise that we have to be agile and adjust quickly – with Covid being the perfect example. We pivoted within weeks of lockdown, with a focus on mental health and resilience, and delivered ten "Ask me anything" calls in the course of five months. We also found ourselves with an opportunity to engage with a rapidly changing discourse on race with the events in the US earlier this year- that led to our largest ever webinar (#IAM) led by the Talk About Black workstream – with about 2,500 people attending, and with social media engagement reaching 60k in a month. It was also great to extend the coverage of our Annual Event this year, which is normally limited to the space of a large auditorium. By going virtual this year, we doubled the number of attendees, and by being more innovative in how we distributed footage of each session, we have been able to leverage content even further.

The DP started as a small group of enthusiastic people; it's now a large group of enthusiastic people. As we've grown, we've got more momentum and that has driven even more enthusiasm. We're now at the stage where we've got so much great information that we're creating, and now the big nut to crack is how do we help the members easily access information and embed new approaches in a way that's appropriate for each company.

When we figure that out, we will be making major, long-term, sustainable change. At the moment, we are just chipping away. Looking back, with ESG, it took quite some time before it reached a tipping point and, suddenly, everybody got it.

What SHOULD companies be working on?

Part of what companies need is step-by-step "how-to" guides that they can follow, and which many find really helpful. This book can play a part in that.

What will drive true long -term change will be culture. But that can be hard (and takes time) to change. Many companies we see think they are truly inclusive when they're not. Having more diverse people in an organisation is great, but really, this is when the journey starts: you then have to ensure that the diverse person doesn't feel isolated, and the rest of the team know how to work with them. It's two sides of the same coin – diversity can't be seen in isolation; you need the inclusion aspect as well.

Are the messages getting through?

Sometimes, I get exhausted and wonder if we are making a difference, but I'm staying positive. I think we are making a difference; the Savings and Investment Industry has now embraced the diversity and inclusions debate, ... but I'd like to make a bigger difference, making long-term sustainable changes, with more companies treating diversity as a business imperative. We need to see cultural changes within organisations that nurture truly inclusive workplaces, to help get better results for customers, provide greater opportunities for diverse talent and create more resilient, successful organisations.

What can YOUR business do to be more diverse and inclusive?

If, like many of us, you have skipped straight to the last section of a book to glean the nuggets, then this is for you!

Over the preceding pages, I have explored a number of the strands of Diversity & Inclusion that every business needs to consider if it is to harness the talents of a wider group of people. But there is undoubtedly a real risk of "D&I Fatigue" setting in if you attempt to go off and tackle all of these issues in one go.

One solution would be to follow the advice on how best to eat an elephant - one bit at a time - and getting to grips with what you might consider the priority areas for your business.

Another is to look at the broader picture and recognise that if you put in place a relatively small number of new practices, you will open up the door to D&I across the piece making everybody feel welcome and wanted in your company. The Diversity Project ask their members to develop a strategy and report on ten keys commitments:

1. We will increase diversity and inclusion training for our employees in order to broaden their understanding and to further raise awareness.

2. We will regularly review, measure and monitor ways in which we can make our company an attractive and accessible place to work for people from a wide range of backgrounds.

3. We will actively support our employees to volunteer their time, knowledge and skills to relevant organisations and social groups, helping to build a more financially informed and secure society.

4. We will have a diversity and inclusion approach, appropriate to the business, which will include measurable wellbeing objectives with the principle of enshrining our belief that good work is safe and inclusive.

5. We will encourage our employees to challenge unconscious bias witnessed amongst their peers.

6. We will build awareness and understanding of mental health perspectives in the workplace.

7. We will measure and monitor the diversity of our employees (e.g., age, gender, ethnicity, sexual orientation, disability) and report this data regularly. We will also encourage open and honest conversations regarding diversity within the workplace and address any underlying issues.

8. We will publicly support and actively contribute to the Diversity Project and other diversity activities (e.g., be involved in two or more Diversity Project workstream initiatives and will be represented at the Steering Committee and/or Advisory Council).

9. We understand that gender differences do matter.

10. We will provide constructive feedback to the Diversity Project where more focus is needed, or a new approach is required.

Appendix
The Diversity Project Charity

100% of the Author's proceeds from this book will be donated to the Diversity Project Charity.

The Diversity Project Charity is a grant-giving organisation. Their initial aim was to raise £2 million to help the charities which had been affected by the President's Club disbandment, as well as some regional charities focussing on inclusivity. From 2020, they will support charities with social mobility, diversity and inclusivity aims. The Charity's grant-giving is guided by a set of values and principles that underpin the work that they do:

Diversity and Inclusion
They believe in empowering people by respecting and appreciating what makes them different, in terms of age, gender, ethnicity, religion, disability, sexual orientation, education, thought and national origin.

Transparency
They ensure they work in an open and honest manner, providing full information required for collaboration and cooperation.

Respect

They seek to act with integrity and value privacy and confidentiality.

Collaboration

They believe in the value of working together and sharing ideas to produce the best results.

Purpose

They want to support and advance charitable causes within the UK and make a positive sustainable impact.

www.diversityprojectcharity.org

About the Author

Steve Butler is a Chartered Manager and Fellow of the Chartered Management Institute. He gained his Master's in Business Administration from Solent University and is currently researching for his Doctorate in Business Administration at the University of Winchester. In his current blended role of business leadership & management, academic researcher, and industry diversity campaigner, he is a regular writer and speaker on intergenerational working, retirement and older worker business management issues. *The Diversity Project: Accelerating progress towards an inclusive culture in the investment and savings industry* is Steve's third management book covering diversity and inclusion issues. Previous books include *Manage the Gap: Achieving success with intergenerational teams* and The Midlife Review*: A guide to work, wealth and wellbeing.*

In 2019, Steve became a member of the Diversity Project Advisory Council and Executive Sponsor of the Smart Working Workstream and is an active supporter of the project. Steve is Chief Executive of Punter Southall Aspire, a national retirement savings business with 150 employees who provide a range of solutions including corporate employee benefit consulting, financial planning advice and telephone-based retirement guidance & advice.

Steve is committed to building a truly incisive workplace within Punter Southall Aspire, demonstrated through their recent Investors in People silver accreditation, Business in the Community Responsible Business Champion Age Award 2020, Management Today NextGen Culture Award 2020, and Reward Strategy D&I Award 2019.